ALEXANDRA and ELIOT ANGLE
photography by ERICKA McCONNELL

cocktail parties
with a twist

DRINKS + FOOD + STYLE

Stewart, Tabori & Chang ▪ New York

Table of Contents

4   INTRODUCTION

THE PARTIES

with recipes

what it's all about

How to throw a party? Wish we could tell you. After years of giving them for friends and designing them for clients, there is only one thing that we truly know: there are no rules. We wish we could give you a simple set of foolproof instructions for hosting the perfect cocktail party or enlighten you to the ten tried-and-true secrets of entertaining. But, alas, we cannot. And what fun would that be, anyway?

What we can give you are tips, ideas, and inspirations gleaned from years of giving and going to parties, both as professionals and for pure pleasure—and show you beautiful images from fourteen of them. These parties are designed to help you discover the two most important things for any host—to find your own style and be confident about expressing it.

This is a book about cocktail parties for our time. Four-course dinners for twelve are great, but the reality is that most of us rarely, if ever, have the time to pull these off successfully. And collegiate-style keg parties with plastic cups where the chips run out just don't cut it anymore, unless you really go for it with irony in hand and a fine eye for detail. The thing is, cocktail parties are what most of us do anyway when we have friends over—we just may not know it.

What this is not is a how-to book. Nor is it a compendium of dinner parties or elaborate galas. We leave that to our predecessors, entertaining gurus that have gone to great lengths to handhold you through every conceivable step of giving a party. What we aim to do is inspire, not merely instruct. To give you a breadth of information that you can chopstick your way through, while never losing sight of the reason we all give parties in the first place—to have fun.

But let's face it: we're all busy people. None of us have the time we did a few generations ago. It would be rare to find someone who has a few weeks to dedicate solely to creating a fabulous fête. After we get home from work at seven, we simply don't have the hours to pull together even a dinner party.

In this book, we try to advocate the simple choice whenever possible, elaborated to its fullest and most creative extent. This is true of everything from menu ingredients to decorations. Simple is fresh, seasonal, straightforward, and glamorous in its honesty. Simple is not processed, affected, or overdone. What we know, what we love is most often how we should present ourselves, what puts us in the best light.

We will show you some of the more traditional customs for making cocktails and hosting successful parties. These may help you to avoid some spills and mishaps, but no perfectly poured martini or appropriately shaped glass can make a party sing. So read on, absorb what you want, experiment a little, and figure out what works for you. Keep in mind that the best parties are often those visited by some fortuitous event or surprising element, something that seems to have occurred without planning or foresight, and even mistakes can be sexy if accomplished with a big smile. So trust your instincts, allow events to unfold naturally, and enjoy the thrill of being surrounded by friends and strangers that are having the best time they've had all month. This, more than anything, is what *Cocktail Parties* is for.

who we are anyway

Aqua Vitae: Events & Interiors is our company. We help people give parties when they want something tremendous for a night. We also design home interiors for people that want to live better on a daily basis. But the best description of what we are about is our name.

Aqua vitae, Latin for "the water of life," was the enthusiastic name first given to alcohol by the fourteenth-century Spanish alchemist Arnoldo de Villanova when he discovered it in his laboratory. He, like most alchemists in his day, had devoted his life to the search for a panacea or "fifth element." When he accidentally produced a crude form of brandy, not only was he sure he had found it but he was flushed and giddy for days and nights on end. He wrote a short book about his discovery, boasting that it "prolongs life, clears away ill humors, revives the heart, and maintains youth." Though with hindsight we know his analysis of alcohol's properties was not entirely clear-headed, it certainly was good-hearted. It is in this spirit of vitality and rosy optimism that we created Aqua Vitae and now this book.

cocktail party: where it all began

The cocktail party itself is actually not that old: the first took place in some of America's larger cities just after the passage of the Eighteenth Amendment in 1920, the "Noble Experiment" that quickly came to be known as Prohibition. Drinking was suddenly both illegal and wildly popular, and society swells decided to gather together to whet their whistles in the privacy of their own homes. This romantic exuberance also gave rise to a revolutionary practice: for the first time, the sexes drank together in public. The presence of the fairer sex placed a premium on the aesthetic, and suddenly everything from cocktails to lounges was created within the framework of well-conceived design. When stylish entertaining took on a new found importance, the cocktail party was born.

The traditional cocktail party is short and early: two and a half hours before dinner. The allotted time is generally based on a triplicate structure: an hour for everyone to be late, an hour for everyone to enjoy themselves, and an hour to kick everybody out. Other than this, the only other requirement for a cocktail party, as tradition defines it, is a focus on mingling and the presence of a few small, well-chilled liquor-based concoctions.

However, the cocktail party, in this traditional form, is awfully hard to pull off unless it's for a formal occasion. After working late, all of us seem to like to get some dinner and then go to a party—not the other way around. A few years ago, we had a running Thursday evening cocktail party in our loft in New York's Tribeca. What we invariably found is that when we invited guests from six to eight, the majority came at nine and stayed until midnight. We never would eat any dinner Thursday evenings (expecting to do so after the party "ended" at eight), and although we always had a fantastic time, we regretted it the next morning when our eyelids seemed glued shut.

We bring this up only to demonstrate that the traditional models often no longer apply. Experiences like this have led us to the somewhat controversial opinion that a cocktail party (or "drinks party," as the English more aptly put it) does not have to take place before dinner to be considered a cocktail party. Cocktail parties are simply what we all do and have done for years—have people over for drinks and just enough food to keep them from leaving. Most of these parties start at ten or eleven and go on for quite a few hours. But they can just as easily take place on a mountaintop at noon or a beach at sunset. The time and place don't matter. The important thing is the desire to mingle, great food and drink, and, we would argue, a pronounced and well-articulated sense of style.

hosting parties

Hosting a party is never easy, it just has to look like it is. Hopefully we can help you recognize that it's one of the simplest and most gratifying pleasures in life. Each of the fourteen chapters that follow contains tips, ideas, and suggestions we've pared down from our years in the business to help you host a party with grace and style. The most important thing to keep in mind is old Arnoldo's maxim: never to stop searching for the water of life.

The water of life, as we see it, is simply what sustains us as humans—not so much food and air, but spirited company and the warmth of good conversation. When a party is truly flowing, when the large majority of those in the room are truly *there*, you have achieved something spectacular and, we think, vital to everyone's very existence. This shouldn't make you apprehensive, but help you to relax and trust your instincts. You should never let nerves or pretensions get in the way of a good time. The only thing that is important, the reason you are bothering with all this in the first place, is to create an atmosphere in which your guests feel free to enjoy themselves with true abandon. Then is when you get a little "aqua vitae" goin' on.

We don't mean to sound New Age-y. In fact, our philosophy is about as old as parties themselves. Not much has changed since we visited our friends, dressed in togas, and laid on divans and took pleasure in wine and each other's company over a lengthy dinner. And we won't even mention the original Bacchanalian revelry that went on in Greece centuries before even that. Everything is possible, you just have to allow it to be.

Here are five hosting tips to help you do just that:

1. **PLAN AHEAD.** The first thing to do when you decide you want to throw a party is sit down and make a list: what is the occasion, how many guests will you invite, how will you let people know about it, what kind of drink and food will you serve, how will you decorate the space? Read all of the recipes and chart out a schedule. A good list is a lifesaver in the hectic final hours.

2. **DON'T OVERDO IT.** Keep the scope of the party possible for you to comfortably accomplish. If you don't have all afternoon free to cook, don't plan on having six different hors d'oeuvres. Focus on a few things or hire pros.

3. **KEEP IT SIMPLE.** The simple choice is often the most elegant. And the most cool, for that matter. Whether it's design or lighting or food choices, it's usually true that simpler is better. Gaudy, baroque adornments can be fun, but most often seem a bit forced—or, that most damning of all descriptives, tacky.

4. **BE SURE TO RELAX.** This is the hardest thing for any host, and the reason most of our clients hire us to throw their parties for them. When giving our own parties, we always take a moment, no matter how unprepared we feel, to sit down together and have a cocktail and a chat just before the first guests arrive.

5. **ENJOY YOURSELF.** Your only important job as a host is to help your guests enjoy themselves. Fact: they will not have a good time if you aren't. Once the festivities have begun, concentrate on remembering only one thing: forgetting. Forget all the lists and planning and schedules and notes and try to have all that girls just want to have—fun.

Remember these things and the rest is easy. Believe us.

food: just do it

The recipes featured are relatively easy to make so that you the host concentrates on the important things—chatting, laughing, and flirting. The repertoire of menu ideas and recipes reinvigorates a few of the standard food categories: the most traditional of cocktail fare, home cooking from around the world, and last-minute blow-out munchies. At Aqua Vitae events, we have found that these are invariably the first to be eaten, even when partnered with the most exotic and elaborate of canapés. Not only are they delicious, simple, and (with a little bit of effort) beautiful, but, perhaps most importantly, they provide the kind of sustenance one needs to accompany the mischievous effects of the cocktail.

At Aqua Vitae, we have developed a set of rules that govern the fare at formal cocktail parties. We created these simply because they make sense: nothing should be larger than one bite (both hands are occupied with the cocktail glass and greeting others and should not be juggling food), no offering should be greasy (greasy fingers leave unattractive marks on the glass and play havoc with perfectly applied lipstick), the food should not crumble (imagine an elegantly dressed lady with crumbs down the front of her silk dress), avoid anything with a bone, toothpick, or skewer (guests never know what to do with them), nothing should be so warm that it burns the fingers or mouth (remember that guests have to be able to snap up any morsel that catches their eye, without gauging the temperature), and most of the food, if not everything, should be passed around the room on platters (keeps everyone lively and, if well executed, ensures that guests feel pampered).

Now that you know our rules, you can set them aside to suit your own sense of style and the party at hand. The fact is, unless you have loads of time and a staff—or a professional caterer—hosting a party that follows all the rules would be impractical, exhausting, and seriously not fun. You will see that we boldly offer a number of recipes for hors d'oeuvres on skewers and even a few that will leave a trace of (only the most delicious) oil on the fingertips. Take these ideas, expand on them as you see fit, and remember the previously mentioned real rules:

Plan ahead. Figure out what you want to serve, read the recipes, and decide if you have time to do everything they require. Remember that there are other things besides cooking that you will want to do in the hours before the party begins—leave plenty of time for dressing and lighting candles and for having that all-important pre-party drink.

Don't overdo it. Make what you know and love, not some chef d'oeuvre you find in a magazine. And don't make anything that keeps you in the kitchen while your guests are there. But don't underdo it either. A cocktail party is not the appropriate time to focus on light foods for weight watchers—you and your guests are there to let your hair down a bit, even if it's on a once-a-month timeline, and you all want real pleasing sustenance.

Keep it simple. One of the most common mistakes that hosts make is to focus too much on the food. Though it may seem like a matter of life and death to you, remember, guests do not come to cocktail parties for the food. They come first to be with their host and to enjoy lively conversation, games, or even a dance with a stranger; and second to enjoy a delicious drink or two complemented by a simple, robust bite to eat. And, with food as with everything else: simple is fresh, simple is seasonal, simple is unprocessed, and simple is comfortable.

cocktail basics

Let's face it: most of us don't get together and play in a string quartet or look at art or discuss literature as much as we might like to. We get together and drink, even if it's just a glass of wine or two. Drink is what it has always been—a social enabler; that which lubricates conversation and intimacy. Instead of overwhelming you with a treatise on the history of partying as it relates to alcohol, we've come up with a number of lists to elucidate what every hostess needs to know about cocktails: what they are and how to make them. In this book we have provided a number of cocktail recipes—some classic and near-forgotten from decades past, but mostly signature drinks we at Aqua Vitae have created for specific events. To distinguish the two, and not take credit for the work of master mixologists, the Aqua Vitae concoctions are followed by the date they were created. And remember, no matter how appealing these beverages are to most, you will have guests that either cannot or will not partake in them. The delight of all the recipes listed is that they can be enjoyed as fine, fresh juices with no alcohol. A nice touch is to lengthen them with a splash of soda and replace any liqueur sweeteners with a simple syrup.

TYPES OF DRINKS

There are several drink families that involve the use of alcohol. The champion of them all is the cocktail.

Cocktails: small 2- to 4-ounce drinks, served well chilled but without ice in a stemmed cocktail glass no larger than 6 ounces, and preferably made with one base liquor and various modifiers.

Highballs: These are the simplest of drinks, composed of one spirit and one mixer (usually soda water or ginger ale) served in a highball glass over ice.

Collinses: Like a Highball, served over ice in a tall Collins glass, they combine any liquor with lemon juice, simple syrup, and soda water.

Sours: Like a Collins, but with no ice or soda, they are one spirit shaken with lemon juice and simple syrup and strained into a sour glass.

Rickeys and Juleps: These are made with one liquor, lime juice, and simple syrup. The Rickey is served over ice in a highball glass, and the Julep with fresh mint in a large julep glass.

Punches: Traditionally made with rum, these are known mostly for their large number of ingredients (they often contain several liquor bases) and for being served out of bowls.

Grogs and Toddies: Usually winter drinks, Grogs are simply heated spirits diluted with water, and Toddies are the same with sugar, spices, and juices added.

Restoratives: What you'll need the morning after if you experiment too much with the above; traditionally made with just one liquor, juices, bitters, spices, ice, and as large a glass as possible.

TYPES OF LIQUOR
distillates from grains:

Whiskey: The grandest liquor family, it encompasses Scotch, Blended Scotch, Irish, Canadian, bourbon, rye, and mash, the differences depending on where it was distilled and what types of grains were used.

Gin: Now considered one of the noblest of liquors despite its common bathtub roots, this is the ultimate cocktail base. Usually English, it's made with a grain base, plus numerous, and often secret, herbs and spices.

Vodka: Distilled from either grain or potatoes, it's usually native to Eastern or Northern Europe.

distillates from plants:

Rum: One of the world's oldest liquors, it's made from sugarcane molasses in the islands of the Caribbean and South America. Rum has the largest range in color and taste of the liquor families, ranging from clear to rich, chocolate brown.

Tequila: Made in Mexico from the agave plant, tequila has enjoyed a newfound popularity in recent years. Silver, Reposado, and Añejo are the three types that enumerate the number of years aged, and often the quality.

Cachaca: The Brazilian equivalent of rum, though distilled directly from the sugarcane itself. Cachaca is the key ingredient in the great Caipirinha, Portuguese for "the drink of farmers."

distillates from wine or other liquors:

Brandy: The other large family of spirits, best known for its famous French twins, Cognac and Armagnac, but also produced in Spain, Portugal, Italy, Germany, Greece, and even the U.S.

Liqueurs: Often employed as a drink modifier (Cointreau, Campari), these are liquors that have been diluted, sweetened, and flavored with herbs and spices.

COCKTAIL EQUIPMENT
What every home bar should have.

Top row, from left:
Shaker: Either metal or glass, this sometimes has the strainer built into the top. We recommend, however, that you use the more old-fashioned Boston shaker, which consists of a metal base with insertable mixing glass.

Bottle and Wine openers: The simpler more old-fashioned design, the better. A lot of these contemporary contraptions that advertise "ease" just take too long for a good bartender.

Strainer: Stainless steel, or silver if you are *très* fancy. Its sole purpose is to keep the ice, besides the occasional lovely shard of ice, out of the drink.

Middle row, from left:
Citrus juicer: Usually the "hand-operated" variety, though an electric juicer comes in handy for Aqua Vitae's signature fresh citrus cocktails.

Swizzle sticks and Bar spoon: The former are merely decorative but fun for guests, whereas the spoon is what a bartender actually uses to make a drink perfectly stirred.

Paring knife and Citrus zesters: Essential for preparing garnishes.

Bottom row, from left:
Ice scoop: To fill your shaker.

Jigger: This is very important equipment. Drink-making is a science, and every real cocktail should be carefully measured with one of these.

Soda siphon: The only way to have fresh soda water.

Not pictured:
Champagne stirrers: For the truly elegant. Eight-pronged extendable stirrers for reviving Champagne bubbles.

Muddler: Needed for the Mojito and other fine drinks to extract essential oils from mint and other herbs.

Clean towels: You never know.

Ice bucket: Preferably insulated to keep cooler.

Ice tongs: Who wants to see your grubby fingers on their cubes?

BAR GLASSES

Glassware is extremely important—it sets the tone of a drink—but almost no hosts have the proper ones for every drink. This is okay, but you should at least know what to aspire to.

Top row, from left:
Tumbler (or Old-Fashioned glass); **Cocktail glass; Water goblet**

Middle row, from left:
Beer Stein; Apéritif glass; Collins glass

Bottom row, from left:
Snifter; Martini glass; Julep glass

Not pictured:
Highball glass; Sour glass (or a Water goblet may do); **Grog or Toddy glass; Champagne flute; Champagne coupe; Wine glasses**

GARNISHES

Garnishes are an essential part of a good drink, yet the "keep it simple" maxim applies more than ever here. We've all been served disastrous tropical drinks with garnishes that seem never to end. The garnish should never overwhelm the drink, but provide the most subtle of accents. Here are the classics:

Twists: Most often from the peel of a lemon, occasionally from the peel of a lime, the twist is the classic and simplest of garnishes, what is served in a true martini. Just slice off a length of peel with a knife, removing the pith, and drop the peel in the drink.

Squeezes: Lime or lemon. It's usually an eighth of the fruit, with the peel on and a slit cut into it.

Wheels: More decorative than not, as they produce little juice, these are slices of citrus that can sit on the rim of the glass.

Green olives

Pearl onions

Maraschino cherries

Mint sprigs

Beyond the tried and true, there is no end to interesting garnishes. Letting the drink's ingredients and the season dictate the options, try anything from sugared raspberries to kumquat slices to cherry tomatoes speared with a cucumber. One of our secrets: Caperberries—a terrific garnish we use in martinis. They have a great salty bite, but are subtle and inventive.

five quick steps to a perfect cocktail

1. Measure ingredients into glass part of shaker.

2. Fill metal part of shaker with ice.

3. Shake vigorously for 8 seconds.

4. Strain into chilled cocktail glass.

5. Garnish and sip up!

cocktail time: how to make them

A proper cocktail is always made up of three parts: the base, the modifier, and the flavoring agent. The base is the one spirit that forms the bulk of the drink. With cocktails, as with nearly all things, remember—you get what you pay for. The more expensive the liquor, the better the drink. It's always better to get less of a good thing and run out, than ply your guests with mediocre booze. So pony up and get the top-shelf spirits.

The modifiers, often called the mixers, are what blend with the base to create a new flavor. Common modifiers are fortified wines (like vermouth), some low-proof spirits (Cointreau), or juices and carbonated waters. With juices, again, the fresher the better. At Aqua Vitae we always hand-make fresh juices the day of the event: their quality and strength of flavor is unmatched by anything in a bottle or can. If you have no option but to use bottled juices, you should test the recipe before serving it to your guests. The drink may have to be modified slightly from our recipe, perhaps with a bit of citrus to enliven the flavor or a bit of simple syrup to sweeten it. Everyone has access to a citrus juicer, so always use fresh lemon, lime, and orange juices. If you don't have time to squeeze before the event, put a hand juicer on the bar. And please do not sink so low as to use "pre-mixed mixers" like sour or margarita mix; these things are extremely easy to make from scratch, and the difference in flavor is astronomical. The most important thing to remember when mixing is that the modifier should never entirely mask the flavor of the base, or original spirit; it should always remain an accent.

The flavoring agent is the third and most delicate of the three parts to any great cocktail. The alteration of the flavor is often extremely subtle, but in a few drops, it can take a drink from decent to sublime. Flavoring agents are the smallest amounts of bitters, herbal liqueurs, liquors or syrups, and they bring a cocktail to completion.

All three of these parts have to be measured to be made. Don't let the most experienced of bartenders fool you, even if it looks like they are free-pouring, they have a system to accurately measure the number of ounces per ingredient. For most of us, the aforementioned jigger is the means of choice. Believe us, there is no shame in taking your time to accurately measure a drink. If anything, it makes you look serious, like you impart the art of drink-making with the respect it deserves. All good drink recipes, and certainly every one in this book, specify their ingredients to an eighth of an ounce. And to not follow them as carefully as you can borders on sacrilege.

Another trick to avoiding embarrassment is the decanting scheme. Most shakers will comfortably prepare two to four cocktails. Any more and they will spill or each glass won't get enough. The trick to pouring, once the drinks have been properly measured and mixed, is to make a pass filling each glass half way up, and then pass back filling each glass up with equal amounts of what remains. That way you don't look the gauche host as your third eager imbiber sighs into his droplets of martini when the other two are grinning and wheeling away as happy as can be.

We've talked about glassware and garnishes, so you at least know which to reach for when it's time to pour. But the last important, and too often overlooked, ingredient in cocktail sculpting is the ice. Having very cold, unmelted fresh ice is the key to any drink. There's nothing worse than a good cocktail made with old, watered-down cubes. Cocktails must be cold to be cocktails: actually, 25°F is just about right. Note that accomplishing this involves changing the ice bucket repeatedly—and throwing out a lot of ice. But taste a cocktail so crisp and fine that it revives every of your senses, and you will know it is indeed well worth it.

well let's get on with it already

All this is what it is: details. Please take all the of above not quite with a grain of salt, but like Arnoldo with a carefree heart and an open mind. We wanted you to know all the etiquette and particulars of drink and food so that it can in some way inform your choices as a host. But remember the five principles and that nothing's worse than a host who is so caught up in following directions that they forget to enjoy themselves and their guests.

A party is never a party if you follow all the rules. Expose and celebrate the beauty of human error once in a while, and you will be a creator of glorious moments and exceptional memories. Think of mistakes as innovations and go into each event with the desire to learn something new, and you will be on your way toward the water of life.

Welcome to the party. Enjoy. Dig in. And when all else fails, blame the caterer.

URBAN loft

The greatest party of the last century was held at the Plaza Hotel at 11 PM on Saturday, November 28, 1966. Or so most of those present attest. Truman Capote's Black & White Ball was remarkable for one thing and one thing only—the guests. Account after account from delirious attendees revealed that the food was unremarkable, the decorations plain, the service tedious, and the music inaudible. What was imminently memorable, what made them feel this was the best party of their lives, was the energy in the room, the delicious privilege of being there. A quality that's hard to pin down, but an essential asset of any truly great party.

Impossible to match? Probably. But what we all should take away from this spectacular coup is that the details don't matter. Almost no one remembers them, even when they are flawlessly and extravagantly executed. What matters is your guest list, certainly. But creating the impression of abandon throughout a room matters even more. This doesn't have to mean wild craziness. Simply that all your guests feel comfortable and happy and, that most elusive of sensations, free from judgment. Able to laugh without a thought. To dance and not think of who's watching. To introduce themselves to strangers. Truman insisted all of his guests wear masks, so that may have given him an advantage. But we can certainly get close to that if we try. Of course, drinks always help. William F. Buckley, Jr. remembers: "A lot of people were pretty lubricated that night, including Truman."

At this light and airy artist's loft in downtown Manhattan we took great care in the look and placement of the bar to make it the focal point of the party. Setting up a bar so it is gorgeous to look at, user friendly, and well placed in the room—for minimal bottleneck and maximum cause for flow—will get any party going. A room should not feel empty and at the same time not feel overcrowded. Once the party begins, concentrate on the flow, the feel, the vibe, let go of all the little things, and you will be well on your way to a place in the stars, or at least on memory lane.

the **guest list**

Whom to invite? This really depends on what kind of party you want to throw—sophisticated, crazy, intelligent, diverse . . . It also depends on numbers, which depends on the space. How many rooms will be used, how many can fit comfortably in them? A party must never feel empty, but guests should be able to sit if they want to or at least move freely and never wait for a drink.

Attractive singles are a must. They give energy to any group. No one likes a party filled with stodgy couples that all live together, especially if you are part of one. Best to invite no one that knows everyone, since introductions are key to any party. Avoid inviting whole groups of friends; save part of the group for the next time. Mix it up.

all the pretty martinis

Martinis come in all shapes and sizes, especially in recent years. But the actual recipe is a true classic that should rarely be fiddled with. (When hostesses want to serve fun, new "martinis," more often than not, what they actually want are cocktails). The tried-and-true Prohibition-era variations are simple, usually involving substitutions in the garnish.

THE ORIGINAL: with a twist of lemon

THE NEAR-AS-CLASSIC: with the ever-popular green olive

THE GIBSON: with a pearl onion rather than the olive

THE BUCKEYE: with a black olive

THE HOMESTEAD: with a slice of orange

THE DIPLOMAT: with a dash of maraschino liqueur

THE DOUGLAS: with both lemon and orange twists

"DIRTY": with a splash of olive brine

"SMOKY": with a dash of scotch

Though any true martini is made with gin, you'll find that many of your guests prefer vodka. Feel free to switch to the Vodkatini popularized by James Bond.

simple syrup

Simple syrup is a key ingredient in many cocktails, particularly those containing a large dose of tart citrus. Simple indeed, it is nothing more than sugar and water. Liquifying the sugar ensures that it mixes seamlessly with the other drink ingredients.

To make simple syrup, mix equal parts sugar and water in a saucepan over low heat. Stir until the sugar has dissolved, about 5 minutes, and remove from heat. Once cooled, you can refrigerate simple syrup in a sealed bottle or jar for up to one week.

There are many delicious variations on simple syrup, some of which you will find in cocktail recipes throughout this book. In summer we always keep a bottle of mint-infused syrup in the refrigerator to flavor fresh lemonade and limeade, and in winter we have a small bottle of vanilla bean–infused syrup ready for morning tea. The possibilities are almost endless.

To make syrup infusions, add the flavoring agent to the cold water and sugar in a saucepan over low heat. Stir for at least 10 minutes until the sugar has dissolved and the syrup is infused with the special ingredient. Remove from heat and cool with the flavoring agent still in the pan. Strain into a bottle or jar, seal, and store.

DRINKS

Green Tea Collins, 2001

For best results, use Matcha or other high-quality powdered green tea in this recipe.

2 ounces vodka
2 ounces strong green tea, cooled
1 ounce fresh lemon juice
1 teaspoon simple syrup (recipe on page 23)
¼ teaspoon grated fresh ginger
Lemon wheel or candied ginger for garnish

Place the vodka, green tea, lemon juice, simple syrup, grated ginger, and plenty of cracked ice in a shaker, and shake vigorously to combine. Strain thoroughly into a Collins glass filled with ice. Garnish with a wheel of lemon or a piece of candied ginger and serve.

Marie Antoinette

The Grande Dame is famous for having commissioned a porcelain factory to make glasses from a cast of her breasts—which later inspired the coupe-shaped champagne glass. The Ritz Hotel in London created this wonderful cocktail in tribute.

4 ounces champagne
½ teaspoon strawberry liqueur
½ teaspoon Calvados
½ teaspoon fresh lemon juice
½ teaspoon Cointreau
Fresh strawberry for garnish

Combine the strawberry liqueur, Calvados, lemon juice, and Cointreau in a shaker, with plenty of cracked ice, and shake vigorously to combine. Strain into a well-chilled champagne flute and top with the champagne. Serve garnished with the fresh strawberry.

Martini

The undisputed heavyweight champion of the world.

3 ounces gin
¼ ounce dry white vermouth
Lemon peel for garnish

Place the gin and vermouth in a shaker, along with plenty of cracked ice, and shake vigorously to combine. Strain into a well-chilled martini glass. Garnish with a lemon twist, or olive if your guest prefers, and serve immediately.

FOOD

Chawan-mushi Eggs

Chawan-mushi, a savory egg custard, is a popular dish in Japan often served as a soup course. Besides its subtle and delicious flavor, chawan-mushi is fantastic for its adaptability—it can be served hot, at room temperature, or even cold.

In this version, we have added shallots, smoked salmon, and dill, but feel free to be inventive with the ingredients. Try adding sliced chicken breast, grated fresh ginger, and lemon zest, or shrimp and sliced shiitake mushrooms. We like to prepare the custard in a separate dish, then serve it in individual eggshells as pictured.

SERVES 10

1 tablespoon sweet butter
l tablespoon finely chopped shallots
¼ pound smoked salmon, coarsely chopped
2 tablespoons finely chopped fresh dill
2 cups light chicken stock, cooled to room
temperature (vegetable stock or Japanese *dashi*
may be substituted)
1 tablespoon mirin (Japanese sweet rice wine)
1 tablespoon soy sauce
4 medium eggs
Fresh dill sprigs, for garnish

In a sauté pan, melt the butter over low heat, add the shallots, and sauté until soft, about 2 minutes. Transfer to a bowl, add the salmon and dill, and toss to combine.

In another bowl, combine the stock, mirin, and soy sauce. Whisk the eggs in a mixing bowl, slowly add the stock mixture, whisking to combine, then add the salmon mixture and stir.

To steam, pour the custard mixture into a heat-resistant vessel—I have used everything from a Pyrex pie dish to a soufflé mold to coffee cups. An easy option is to steam and serve the finished dish in ceramic or glass juice or shot glasses. Just pour the custard mixture directly into the glasses, cover each one with plastic wrap or foil, and place in a hot steamer. Cover and steam for 15 minutes or until the custard sets (the time will vary depending on the size of the glasses you are steaming). Remove the chawan-mushi from the steamer, cool to desired serving temperature, and serve accompanied by a small spoon (see Note). Garnish with a sprig of dill.

NOTE: If you want to serve your chawan-mushi in eggshells, we recommend that you invest in an egg topper. Just slice the tops off the eggshells, drain the contents and rinse, then refill the eggshells with the custard. Serve the custards in egg cups or balanced in piles of rock salt, pebbles, or rice.

Belgian Endive with Tuna Tartare

It is very important that the fish is sashimi quality and very fresh. Although tuna freezes better than most fish, there is no question that freezing sorely damages the flavor. If you cannot find adequately fresh tuna steak in your local market, consider using boiled and chopped shrimp as a substitute.

MAKES 30 PIECES

3 large Belgian endive (about ¾ pound)
¾ pound sashimi-quality tuna steak
2 tablespoons fresh lemon juice
1 tablespoon rice vinegar
2 tablespoons soy sauce
½ teaspoon sesame oil
½ teaspoon sugar
½ teaspoon grated fresh ginger

Carefully peel the leaves of the endive so they remain intact. Rinse, pat dry, and refrigerate. Rinse the tuna, pat dry, and cut into ¼-inch cubes. Transfer to a bowl, cover, and refrigerate. Whisk the lemon juice, rice vinegar, soy sauce, sesame oil, sugar, and ginger in a small bowl to create a sauce; set aside.

When serving time is near, pour the sauce over the tuna. Arrange the endive leaves on a serving platter and fill each leaf with a tablespoon or two of the tuna tartare. Cover the hors d'oeuvres with a slightly damp cloth and return them to the refrigerator until just before serving.

Two Tartlets:
STEAK TERIYAKI and SPINACH WITH SWEET MISO

Tartlets are one of our favorite things to serve at any party. The shells can be made in advance (if stored in the freezer, up to a month!). They always look delicate and beautiful, and the variations on the fillings are endless. Here we share two of our favorite versions, both with a Japanese twist, but you should feel free to experiment with your own fillings.

Tartlet Shells

MAKES 3 DOZEN 2-INCH TARTLETS

2½ cups all-purpose flour
1 teaspoon salt
16 tablespoons sweet butter
½ cup ice water

Combine the flour, salt, and butter in a food processor, and pulse until a coarse, crumbly dough forms. Add the ice water to the dough and continue pulsing until well mixed. Form the dough into a ball, wrap securely in plastic wrap, and refrigerate until firm, about 2 hours. (At this point, the dough can be placed in a sealed plastic bag, and frozen for up to one month. Just place in the refrigerator for 2 hours to thaw before baking.)

When ready to bake, preheat the oven to 400°F. Remove half the dough from the refrigerator, transfer to a flat, floured surface, and roll out the dough until ¼- to ⅛-inch thick. With a glass or cookie cutter, cut circles out of the dough that are slightly larger than the 2-inch tartlet molds. (You should have about 38 circles.) Press each circle into a tartlet mold and pinch off any excess that hangs over the edges. Pierce the bottom of each tartlet with a fork or toothpick and put them in the freezer for about 10 minutes to rechill the dough.

When the dough is firm again, bake the tartlets for 10 to 12 minutes, until they are a very light gold. Cool on wire racks before carefully turning out of the molds. Repeat the process with the remaining dough. At this point, the tartlets may be filled with the steak teriyaki or spinach with sweet miso mixtures and served, or they may be transferred to an airtight container and refrigerated for up to one week or frozen for up to one month.

Steak Teriyaki Filling

FILLS 3 DOZEN TARTLETS

3 tablespoons prepared honey mustard
1½ tablespoons wasabi paste*
1½ tablespoons vegetable oil
2 pounds sirloin steak
3 tablespoons sake or dry white wine
3 tablespoons mirin (Japanese sweet rice wine)
1½ tablespoons soy sauce
*Available at Asian grocers or specialty food stores

Combine the honey mustard and wasabi in a small dish to form a sauce; set aside.

Heat the oil in a skillet over high heat. Fry the steak for 3 minutes or until it's seared. Flip the steak, pour the sake over it, cover, and continue to cook for 5 minutes or until the sake has cooked off. Remove the steak from the skillet and set aside.

Add the mirin and soy sauce to the skillet and bring to a boil over high heat. Return the steak to the skillet, and cook 30 seconds more on each side. Remove from the pan and coarsely chop. Fill each shell with 1 to 2 tablespoons steak teriyaki, and top with a small dollop of the honey-mustard sauce. Serve hot or at room temperature.

Spinach with Sweet Miso Filling

FILLS 3 DOZEN TARTLETS

4 cups boiled spinach (3 bags of fresh spinach)
6 tablespoons sweet white miso
1½ tablespoon mirin (Japanese sweet rice wine)
3 teaspoons rice vinegar
1½ teaspoons salt
1½ teaspoons sugar
3 tablespoons water
4 large eggs, beaten (optional)
⅔ cup heavy cream (optional)

Squeeze the excess water out of the spinach, then finely chop or puree; set aside. In a saucepan over low heat, whisk together the miso, mirin, vinegar, salt, sugar, and water until a smooth sauce forms. Add the spinach and toss to combine. If you want to serve a vegan version, fill each tartlet shell with 1 to 2 tablespoons of the mixture now. Transfer the tartlets to a baking sheet, cover with foil, and keep warm in the oven until serving time.

If you want to create a richer filling, first preheat the oven to 350°F. Add the eggs and cream to the skillet and stir to combine. Spoon 1 to 2 tablespoons filling into each of the tartlet shells, transfer to a baking sheet, cover with foil, and bake for 10 minutes or until the mixture has set. Remove the foil, bake for 2 minutes longer, then serve.

impossibly

SMALL

APARTMENT

Everyone at some point at the youthful end of their spectrum has lived in one of those apartments that seems too small even to consider entertaining, much less pull off a party. What do you do, never have people over? Content yourself with your friends' attempts at hosting? Of course not.

Eliot lived in the tiniest of tiny apartments in Paris. A little attic hovel tucked somewhere above Montmartre. From the center of the one-room space, you felt that you could touch every surface without moving both feet. But repositioning the bed and making it a couch, turning the windowsill into a makeshift bar, and clearing everything else out of the room made it an ideal space for the local caférati to mingle. Alexandra had one of these in Tokyo. True, the Japanese are accustomed to maximizing small spaces, but throw a few pillows on the floor and you could have a cozy little conversation nook.

You want to have people over for drinks and have 400 square feet to do it in. The layout and location are immaterial. The most important thing is, once you've made a few arrangements to make the space simple and clear, treat your garret as a chateau. If you see it this way, your guests will invariably follow suit. Have some fun—make everyone dress for a change. Send formal invitations. Splurge on ridiculously expensive champagne. Whatever makes the party feel like a celebration to you. And let the games begin.

bar essentials: what **you** absolutely **can't** live **without**

As the photographer H. i. Williams noted in his 1943 book *3 Bottle Bar*, "There is one simple rule to remember in stocking your bar and that is that acceptable cocktails, or other drinks, do not emerge from poor ingredients." So buy the good stuff.

LIQUORS (the standards are vodka, gin, tequila, whiskey, and rum—though often the first three are more than enough)

DRY WHITE WINE and **VERMOUTH**

SIMPLE SYRUP

CITRUS (limes, lemons, oranges)

GARNISHES (olives, maraschino cherries, and then some)

BITTERS

FRESH MINT

living large

The most intimate setting for a party is a small space. Remember that people tend to be happiest when close to others. So love your lack of extra space.

● Clean up. Clutter can be the death of design, and in the case of a small space, it's the death of comfort as well. So spend some time putting things away.

● Use a desk or a closet as the bar (drape it with fabric if you want), or put the bar in the doorway of a room that you won't be using.

● Use your bed as a coatrack, or if you live in a studio, cover it with a heavy cloth and lots of pillows to create a three-sided couch.

● Push the dining table, desk, and any stray chairs against the wall to open up the central space. Make sure to preserve a few cozy little seating areas for semi-private gossiping.

fresh fruit juice

Store-bought juices are the instant coffee of the cocktail world. Any serious host should at least have a citrus juicer. To make a full range of seasonal, fresh cocktails, though, you need a fruit and vegetable juicer. There are many affordable ones on the market, and juicing with almost all fruits with these machines couldn't be easier: just cut up in small pieces and throw in.

But remember to always sample your juice before mixing. You may find that the fruits you juiced were not perfectly ripe and require a bit of simple syrup or a dash of Cointreau to sweeten them, or that they were overripe and need a squeeze of citrus to bring them back to life. We always strain our juices, including citrus juice: this makes a cleaner cocktail. You should figure out your preference and go with it.

We understand that at times it may be difficult to make or purchase some of the fresh fruit juices that Aqua Vitae drinks require. With that in mind, we have given you an acceptable alternative to the real thing in a number of our recipes. Some techniques you can try when the juice simply isn't available:

- **Simmering berries (even frozen can work here) in water at a ratio of 1:1 over low heat for 15 minutes or more can produce a good result. Strain, then add sugar and citrus to taste.**

- **Melons and mango may be pureed, although the resulting substance can be quite thick. If you want something closer to juice, let the puree settle then scoop off the pulp that rises to the top, or leave it thick and make a frozen version of the cocktail in a blender.**

To make the berry mixer, puree the berries in a blender with the water and the simple syrup. Thoroughly strain the mixture through a cheesecloth or very fine sieve. Makes about 20 ounces juice mix.

Place the vodka, Chambord, juice mixture (or Fresh Berry Mixer), lime juice, and plenty of cracked ice in a shaker, and shake vigorously to combine. Strain into a highball glass filled with ice. Add the ginger ale, garnish with the fresh berries, and serve.

Mango Margarita

A delicious variation on the popular classic. If you cannot obtain the fresh stuff, you can substitute a mango puree for the juice.

1½ ounces tequila
½ ounce Cointreau
2 ounces fresh mango juice (see Fresh Fruit Juice, page 33) or Fresh Mango Mixer
½ ounce fresh lime juice
Cayenne pepper and kosher salt for garnish
Lime wedge for garnish

FOR THE FRESH MANGO MIXER:
1 medium-sized ripe mango

To make the mango mixer, peel and roughly chop the mango, discarding the pit. Puree in a blender, adding water to thin puree, if desired. Makes about 8 ounces puree.

Place the tequila, Cointreau, mango juice or mango mixer, lime juice, and plenty of cracked ice in a shaker, and shake vigorously to combine.

Combine 1 part cayenne to 8 parts salt in a small dish. Lightly rub the rim of a well-chilled glass with the lime wedge, then dip it in the cayenne-salt mixture to coat. Strain into the glass and serve.

DRINKS

Neptune's Nectar, 2001

FOR THE COCKTAILS:
2 ounces vodka
½ ounce Chambord
1 ounce mixed fresh blackberry and raspberry juice (see Fresh Fruit Juice, page 33) or Fresh Berry Mixer
½ ounce fresh lime juice
Ginger ale
Fresh blackberries and raspberries for garnish

FOR THE FRESH BERRY MIXER:
12 ounces mixed fresh or frozen blackberries and raspberries
⅓ cup simple syrup (recipe on page 23)
1 cup water

Pimm's and Soda

This fabulous English summertime drink is perfect for punting on the Thames or any other occasion.

2 ounces Pimm's
½ ounce fresh lemon juice
Soda water
Peeled cucumber stick for garnish

Place the Pimm's and lemon juice in a shaker and shake vigorously to combine. Strain into a highball glass filled with ice, and finish with soda water. Garnish with the cucumber swizzler and serve.
(For photo, see page 34.)

FOOD

Jicama Slices with Avocado and Crab Salad

We will serve almost anything on jicama slices—their light, sweet, and refreshing crunch makes everything taste a bit brighter.

MAKES ABOUT 2 ½ CUPS SALAD PLUS CRUDITÉS FOR DIPPING

1 large jicama (about 1½ pounds)
2 medium-size ripe avocados
¾ cup chopped tomato
½ cup diced red or yellow bell pepper
1 tablespoon minced jalapeño pepper
1 teaspoon salt
2 teaspoons fresh lemon juice
½ cup fresh crabmeat

Peel and slice the jicama into 1- by 3-inch strips about ⅛-inch thick; you should have 20 to 24 slices total. Cover with a damp towel and set aside.

Cut the avocados in half and remove the pits. Scoop the pulp into a bowl and mash with a fork. Add the tomato, bell pepper, jalapeño, salt, and lemon juice, and mix well. Taste and adjust the salt and lemon juice. Stir in the crabmeat.

Spread 1 tablespoon of the salad on each jicama slice, or serve as a dip with jicama as the crudité. This is not a make-ahead dish.

VARIATION: We served a vegetarian version at our party, adding everything but the crabmeat to the dip.

Ceviche on Corn Crisps

In order to taste the real corn flavor, prepare these chips fresh. They are easy to prepare and the flavor is far superior to anything available in a bag.

Always use the freshest seafood when making ceviche, or if you are unsure how fresh it is, lightly cook the seafood before combining with the other ingredients. In this recipe we use a white fish, but many types of seafood are appropriate—from fish to scallops or shrimp.

MAKES ABOUT 2 CUPS CEVICHE PLUS ONE GOOD-SIZED BOWL OF CHIPS

FOR THE CRISPS:
15 corn tortillas
2 tablespoons vegetable oil
1 teaspoon salt

FOR THE CEVICHE:
1 medium cucumber, peeled, seeded, and diced
2 teaspoons salt
1 pound skinless mahi mahi, red snapper, or
    another firm white fish
⅓ cup fresh lime juice
½ cup minced red onion
¼ cup fresh cilantro
1 tablespoon grated orange zest
2 teaspoons grated fresh ginger
2 teaspoons minced serrano chili pepper
Salt to taste

Brush each of the tortillas very lightly with the oil and salt. Use a cookie cutter or small knife to cut the tortillas into bite-size pieces. Warm a cast-iron pan over low to medium heat and lightly toast the tortilla pieces, about 1 minute on each side. Remove from heat and cool.

Sprinkle the cucumber with salt and let stand for 30 minutes. Rinse well, drain, and pat dry. Cut the fish into ½-inch cubes and place in a plastic or glass bowl. Add the cucumber, lime juice, onion, cilantro, orange zest, ginger, and chili pepper. Cover and refrigerate, stirring every 30 minutes, until the fish is opaque and quite firm, 1 to 2 hours. Salt the ceviche if desired and serve cold on the tortilla crisps.

Steamed–Chicken Rice Balls with Dipping Sauce

These hors d'oeuvres can be prepared a day or even a week in advance and refrigerated until it's time to steam and serve. Do not wait until the last minute because they need to chill for at least an hour before steaming.

MAKES ABOUT 24 PIECES PLUS SAUCE

FOR THE RICE BALLS:

1 cup uncooked short-grain white rice

1 pound ground chicken

1 egg, well beaten

¾ cup finely chopped onion

1 can (8 ounces) water chestnuts, finely chopped

5 pickled jalapeños, minced

¼ cup chopped fresh cilantro

1 tablespoon salt

Lettuce or cabbage leaves to prevent rice balls from sticking

FOR THE DIPPING SAUCE:

6 tablespoons soy sauce

2 tablespoons fresh lime juice

2 teaspoons simple syrup (recipe on page 23)

Rinse rice and soak for 2 to 3 hours. Drain and set aside.

Mix together the chicken, egg, onion, water chestnuts, jalapeños, cilantro, and salt in a bowl. Shape into 24 one-inch balls.

Cover a baking sheet with wax paper. Spread the rice onto a flat surface and roll the balls of chicken to coat with rice. Place the rice balls on the wax paper, cover with a second piece of wax paper, and refrigerate or freeze for at least 1 hour. Once chilled, you can transfer the rice balls to an airtight container, separating them with layers of wax paper, and refrigerate or freeze for future use.

When it's almost time to serve, boil water in a pot or the bottom half of a steamer. Line the steaming basket or top half of the steamer with the lettuce leaves, place the rice balls on top of the lettuce, cover, and steam over a rolling boil for about 30 minutes.

To make the dipping sauce, stir together the soy sauce, lime juice, and simple syrup. Serve in a small bowl alongside the rice balls.

DOCK at sunset

When Isabella Stewart moved to Boston in 1860

to marry Alexandra's great-great-great-uncle John Lowell Gardner, Jr., she didn't have a lot going for her. Barely twenty-two, from a "new" wealthy family from New York City of all places, with no friends or relatives nearby, she entered into one of Massachusetts' oldest and most prominent families. To say she was given the cold shoulder is an especially apt depiction of Boston society of the time, and in fact she more or less took to bed for a year or two. But a few years later, after returning from a European tour, she resurrected herself with society through sheer will, and soon was not only a world-class art collector, but the hostess of the most sought-after salon in the city.

If anything can be said about Aunt Belle's entertaining, it is that she wasn't afraid to follow her instincts. She was known for wearing scandalous French fashions and for giving lavish themed parties and spectacles in unusual places. She surrounded herself with artists and musicians and the cream of society alike. Conservative Boston didn't know quite what to make of her, but they followed in her wake. As the gossip magazine *Town Topics* reported in 1887, "Mrs. Jack, as she is familiarly called, is easily the brightest and breeziest woman in Boston, the idol of the men and the envy of the women. . . . Let the wives of giddy and wayward husbands scold and stamp their feet, the spell of Mrs. Jack's enthrallment cannot be broken."

Exaggeration, no doubt. But what she was able to do, against notable odds, was grab the small and closed society world of Boston by its horns and show them a good time. She entertained with zest and a relish for the new and unexpected and, above all, a sense of fun. She gave parties and concerts in fields, on boats, and in the museum she so meticulously designed later in life. Anywhere that seemed fun and spontaneous. Her presence is still felt on the family island we visit in Maine. Its raw natural beauty made it a perfect backdrop for her entertaining, as it does for us now. It is with a humble nod to her enthusiasm that we organized this cocktail party on the end of the dock, in full view of a spectacular sunset, a few steps from the birch grove to which she gave her name.

alternative
spaces

One of the surest ways to make a simple party a real occasion is to have it in an unusual place. Expectations get notched up a rung, and your guests will be excited and ready for the event. This space might be a dock in the middle of nowhere, in your local park, on a roof, or at the top of a hill. The place really doesn't matter, just the sense of beauty and drama that it inspires.

outdoor

parties

- Have a contingency plan for poor weather.

- Note on invitations that the party is outside so guests know what to wear.

- Keep some shawls, throws, and light sweaters around for your guests in case it cools off.

- Place rocks in the bottom of vases to prevent them from tipping over in the wind. Weight down napkins with heavy items.

- Position plenty of citronella and lavender candles to keep the bugs away.

- There's no reason not to use glass glasses and linen napkins just because you are outside. Your guests will always appreciate the extra effort and aesthetic pleasure if you never skimp on the essentials, no matter where you are.

many **drinks**
for many
people

You will have noticed that all the recipes in this book, with the exception of a few punches, yield one cocktail. We all know that it is not always possible to hire a bartender, and it can get tedious being trapped behind the bar while guests demand a few more of those "special drinks." On these occasions, set up a guest-friendly bar, and eliminate as many intricate steps in your drinks as possible. We often carefully mix all the ingredients (save the base alcohol) in a lovely pitcher, then place it on the bar alongside a card with the drink-mixing instructions. This will free you up to mingle, and still ensure that guests imbibe to their palates' delight.

DRINKS

Berry Patch, 1999

FOR THE COCKTAILS:
1½ ounces vodka
½ ounce Limoncello
3 ounces fresh strawberry juice (see Fresh Fruit
  Juice, page 33) or 5 ripe strawberries
2 fresh mint leaves
Sprig of fresh mint for garnish

Place the vodka, Limoncello, juice or ripe strawberries (see Note), and plenty of cracked ice in a shaker, and shake vigorously to combine. Rub the rim of a well-chilled cocktail glass with the mint leaves. Strain the contents of the shaker into the glass and garnish with the sprig of mint.

NOTE: If you cannot find fresh strawberry juice, hull and slice 5 fresh strawberries, puree them in a blender, and strain each cocktail with extra care.

Kiwi Whiskey Sour, 1999

1½ ounces bourbon
1 ounce fresh kiwi juice (see Fresh Fruit Juice,
  page 33)
¼ ounce simple syrup (recipe on page 23)
¼ ounce fresh lemon juice
Fresh cherry (with stem) for garnish

Place the bourbon, kiwi juice, simple syrup, lemon juice, and plenty of cracked ice in a shaker, and shake vigorously to combine. Strain into a sour glass, garnish with the cherry, and serve.

Peabody Punch

One of Alexandra's Peabody ancestors created this punch during his travels, and the recipe has stayed in the family for generations. We can say from experience that it's not for the faint of heart.

SERVES 20

10 ounces guava jelly*
1 dozen large limes or 2 dozen small limes
½ cup superfine sugar plus more to taste
2 cups green tea
24 ounces rum
12 ounces cognac
6 ounces Madeira
Ginger ale or soda water (optional)

*If you can't find this at your supermarket, visit a specialty food store or Latin American market.

Boil 2 cups water in a medium saucepan and add the guava jelly, stirring until it dissolves. Set aside to cool.

Roll the whole, unpeeled limes in the sugar to flavor it with lime essence. Dissolve two thirds of the sugar in the tea. Cut the limes in half and squeeze their juice into a large pitcher. Add the remaining sugar to the lime juice and stir until it dissolves. Add the cooled guava mixture and green tea and mix well to combine. Add more sugar, if desired.

Pour the contents of the pitcher into a large punch bowl and add the rum, cognac, and Madeira, stirring to combine. Allow to stand for at least 12 hours—24 is better. This punch improves with age and may be made 4 weeks in advance. When ready to serve, float a block of ice in the center of the punch bowl. If you want to weaken the concoction a little, serve in a Collins glass topped with ginger ale or soda water.

FOOD

Roasted Pepper and Feta Canapés

MAKES 30 PIECES

3 medium bell peppers (about 1¼ pounds)
1 tablespoon olive oil
1 tablespoon red wine vinegar
½ teaspoon salt
1 teaspoon chopped fresh oregano
½ pound feta cheese, crumbled
½ cup kalamata olives, pitted and cut into slivers
Yolks from 2 boiled eggs (optional)
Salt to taste (optional)

30 crackers or slices grilled crusty bread

Preheat the broiler. Cut the peppers in half lengthwise, discarding the seeds and membranes. Place the pepper halves, skin side up, on a foil-lined baking sheet; flatten using your hand. Broil 3 inches from heat for 12 minutes or until the skin is blackened. Place the peppers in a paper bag; seal and let stand for 15 minutes.

When the peppers have cooled, peel and discard the skins, then slice into thin slivers. Whisk together the oil, vinegar, salt, and oregano in a bowl. Add the pepper slivers and marinate for at least 30 minutes. The pepper mixture can be refrigerated in the marinade for up to a week or used immediately.

To assemble the canapés the day of the party, layer the feta cheese, marinated peppers, and olives on top of the crackers. Chop the egg yolks, sprinkle with salt, and place on top of each canapé, if desired.

Eggplant Caviar with Garlic Pita Crisps

A tasty alternative to crackers, these crisps can be made a day or so in advance and stored in an airtight container. If you are not a garlic fan, try sprinkling these with your favorite herbs before toasting.

MAKES ABOUT 1½ CUPS CAVIAR
PLUS 32 CRISPS

FOR THE CAVIAR:
1 large eggplant (about 1½ pounds)
3 tablespoons good-quality olive oil
½ cup finely chopped onion
2 tablespoons tomato paste
2 tablespoons water
2 teaspoons fresh lemon juice
1 teaspoon salt
Pepper to taste

FOR THE CRISPS:
2 pieces pita bread
2 tablespoons olive oil
Salt to taste
2 medium cloves garlic, peeled

To make the caviar, bring water to boil in a pot large enough to submerge the entire eggplant. Immerse the eggplant in the boiling water and cook for 30 minutes. Remove and set aside to cool. Once cooled, stem, peel, and coarsely chop. Set aside.

Heat 1 tablespoon of the oil in a skillet over medium heat and sauté the onion for 8 minutes. Reduce heat and add the tomato paste, water, and eggplant. Cook, stirring occasionally, for 15 minutes until most of the liquid evaporates. Add the remaining 2 table-spoons oil and continue cooking, uncovered, until the mixture is quite thick. The total cooking time depends on the size of the eggplant, but it should

take about an hour. Remove from heat, add the lemon juice, salt, and pepper to taste. Chill for 2 to 3 hours or overnight.

To make the crisps, preheat the oven to 350°F. Split each pita in half to make two large pita circles, then slice each half into eight thin wedges or use a cookie cutter to make special shapes. Place the pita pieces on two nonstick baking sheets, brush the tops with the oil, and sprinkle with the salt. Bake for 5 minutes or until lightly toasted. Flip and toast the other side of the wedges for another 3 minutes. Remove from the oven and lightly rub the garlic cloves over one side of each crisp. Serve warm with the eggplant caviar.

Spring Lamb Puffs with Lemon-Yogurt Dip

MAKES ABOUT 24 PIECES PLUS DIP

FOR THE LAMB PUFFS:
1 tablespoon olive oil
½ cup chopped onion
1 pound ground lamb
1 tablespoon tomato paste
¼ cup red wine
2 tablespoons fresh chopped parsley
2 teaspoons salt
16 ounces frozen puff pastry dough, thawed
2 eggs

FOR THE DIP:
½ cup whole-milk yogurt
1 teaspoon fresh lemon juice
½ teaspoon grated lemon zest
⅛ teaspoon paprika
⅛ teaspoon cumin
½ teaspoon salt

Preheat the oven to 400°F.

Heat the oil in a sauté pan over medium heat. Add the onion and cook until translucent, about 3 minutes. Add the lamb and cook, breaking the meat up with a wooden spoon, until browned, about 10 minutes.

Combine the tomato paste, red wine, parsley, and salt in a bowl. Add the wine mixture to the lamb and simmer until the liquid has evaporated, about 15 minutes. Remove from heat and set aside.

Separate the two layers of puff pastry dough and, on a lightly floured surface, roll out the dough until ⅛-inch thick. Using a 4-inch cookie cutter, cut out 24 circles. Place about 1½ tablespoons lamb mixture in the center of each circle of dough. Whisk the eggs in a bowl and brush the edges of the circles with the egg. Fold the circles in half, press the edges to seal in the lamb mixture, and place on a nonstick or lightly greased baking sheet. Brush the top of each puff with egg and bake for 15 minutes or until puffy and golden brown.

To make the dip, combine the yogurt, lemon juice, lemon zest, paprika, cumin, and salt, then chill for at least 1 hour. Serve in a small bowl to accompany the lamb puffs. The dip can be made the night before the party or be chilled for a few hours; the lamb puffs should be served warm.

FIRST-HOUSE
gathering

Our first house, bought on nothing more than a lark, was a tiny, ramshackle, eighteenth-century farmhouse outside a small seaside town in Maine. It was wonderfully rustic, utterly private, and completely charming—so much so, in fact, that it took us a number of weeks to realize that we had no need for it whatsoever. That said, there is something about a first house that stays with you. You remember every detail; the little improvements you make seem Herculean in scope. We had terrific weekends there for about nine months, until we planned to move to London and parted ways.

Everyone loves a first house; no one loves to move in. We've found that a great work (and tension) reliever is to have a moving-in party. Grab some friends, pitch camp outside, and spend the day with paint rollers, vacuums, and loud loud music. Just because there are boxes every-where doesn't mean you make no effort to make it beautiful for your guests. It's like any other party; more so, in fact, as you're enticing your guests to work. So, unpack your fun old glasses, order some tasty takeout, and make it feel like the event that it is.

And trust us, they will want to come back again and again.

hors d'oeuvres:
the quantities

This depends on the number of people you are having over and the lavishness of the spread. In general, figure that each of your guests will consume two or three of each of the hors d'oeuvres. For a group of ten to fifteen, you will want three or four varieties, for fifteen to twenty-five guests, offer four or five, and for twenty-five plus offer five or more kinds of hors d'oeuvres.

the music

Music is one of the primary means to set the mood at a party so choose it carefully. Burn a CD or make a mixed tape in advance, or enlist the support of a wannabe dj friend. The music should generally progress in volume with the evening—beginning comfortably for conversation and ending with dancing, if that is your wish. Place the speakers outside of the seating areas—this is where people congregate to chat, and they need to be able to hear each other.

dressing up
takeout

Take-out food is a marvelous thing, and you should always be willing to take advantage of it, particularly if it makes you a less-stressed host. The only key is to remember presentation. One of the best dinner parties we've been to was a form of potluck takeout where each of the guests brought their favorite dish from their favorite restaurant. The results were spectacular, and everyone ate very very well.

There are a few things you can do to enhance the taste of takeout. Enliven the flavor by chopping and adding:

FRESH HERBS

VIDALIA or **RED ONIONS**

TOMATOES

DICED CUCUMBERS

a sprinkle of **OLIVE OIL** or a squeeze
   of **LEMON** or **LIME**

And to improve the presentation, try:

- **Wrapping it in lettuce, basil, or mint leaves**
- **Serving it on a slice of cucumber or apple**
- **Sprinkling it with the petals of edible flowers**
- **Serving it on your finest china**

DRINKS

Slippery Fish, 2000

2 ounces dark rum
2 ounces fresh orange juice
½ ounce fresh lime juice
4 ounces ginger beer
Orange wedge for garnish

Place the rum, orange and lime juices, and plenty of cracked ice in a shaker, and shake vigorously to combine. Strain into a tumbler filled with ice, and top with the ginger beer. Serve with the orange wedge as garnish.

Banana Daiquiri

Bring your sense of humor and forget about dessert!

3 ounces dark rum
1 ounce banana liqueur
2 teaspoons molasses
1 ounce fresh lime juice
1 peeled fully ripe banana
1 to 2 cups ice

Combine all the ingredients in a blender and puree until smooth and thick, adjusting the quantity of ice as necessary. Serve in a highball glass or large water goblet with a straw.

Citrus Shandy

This is a variation on the great English classic.

8 ounces beer (we prefer amber ale)
4 ounces ginger beer or ginger ale
½ ounce fresh lemon juice
Lemon wheel for garnish (optional)

Chill all the ingredients, then combine them in a large beer mug and serve. Garnish with a lemon wheel, if desired.

FOOD

Fresh Garden Pickles

This easy-to-make finger food has a great crunch and is the perfect accompaniment to pressed sandwiches. All you need to make these pickles is a large bowl and a sauté pan. Don't feel hampered by our choice of vegetables—the options are limited only by what you can find fresh.

MAKES 6 CUPS

1 medium cucumber, cut into 16 spears
1 tablespoon kosher salt
2 tablespoons olive oil
16 asparagus spears, cleaned
6 medium carrots, peeled and cut in half
1 medium red bell pepper, cut into 16 slices
1 medium red onion, cut into 16 slices
2 tablespoons pressed or finely chopped garlic
1 tablespoon fresh oregano
1 tablespoon fresh thyme
1 teaspoon crushed black peppercorns
1 cup white wine vinegar
¼ cup balsamic vinegar
2 tablespoons sugar
2 teaspoons fennel seeds
2 bay leaves, crumbled

In a mixing bowl, toss the cucumbers with salt to coat, then cover with ice cubes and refrigerate. After 1 to 2 hours, drain, rinse thoroughly, and strain to remove excess water. Set aside.

In a sauté pan, heat the olive oil over medium heat. Add the asparagus, carrots, peppers, onions, and garlic and sauté for 3 minutes or until the vegetables are just beginning to soften. Transfer to a large bowl. Add the cucumbers, oregano, thyme, and peppercorns and gently toss to combine.

Return the sauté pan to medium heat, and add the vinegars, sugar, fennel seeds, and bay leaves. Simmer until the sugar has dissolved, stirring constantly, about 3 minutes. Pour the syrup over the vegetable mixture and toss to coat. Cool to room temperature, then cover and refrigerate. These pickles are best a few days after they have been made, but can be eaten after chilling for just a few hours.

Pressed Caprese Sandwiches

Reminiscent of a classic grilled cheese sandwich, these pressed sandwiches are very popular with our friends. If you serve enough of them, they can take the place of a light meal.

MAKES 16 SMALL TEA SANDWICHES

2 large tomatoes
2 tablespoons balsamic vinegar
½ teaspoon salt
½ teaspoon pepper
1 pound fresh mozzarella (we love smoked
but plain will do)
16 pieces thinly sliced white bread
Olive oil to brush on bread
16 fresh basil leaves

Thinly slice the tomatoes and dress with the balsamic vinegar, salt, and pepper. Thinly slice the mozzarella. Brush one side of each piece of bread with olive oil. Place a slice of mozzarella, two basil leaves, and a slice or two of tomato between the bread slices, oiled sides out.

Heat a frying pan over medium-high heat. Add as many sandwiches as will comfortably fit in the pan, then cover with a flat top that is slightly smaller than the pan. Cook for 3 minutes or until the cheese melts, applying pressure to the top for 1 minute to flatten the sandwiches. Flip the sandwiches and repeat the process on the other side. Repeat until all the sandwiches are cooked. Cut in half on the diagonal, cover with foil, and keep warm in the oven until ready to serve.

NOTE: We prefer to serve this hors d'oeuvre as a small canapé. Use a cookie cutter to make crustless 1½-inch squares, then cut these on a diagonal as pictured.

glamour by
the POOL'S EDGE

Abandon. About as delicious as a word can be,
it brings up all sorts of associations. Play. Pleasure. Carefreeness. Exuberance. Excess. It's everything you want at a party, and what you rarely encounter. "Hail, high Excess—especially in wine/ To thee in worship do I bend the knee," wrote Ambrose Bierce.

Do you remember going to parties as a child? Screaming and running around in circles and throwing things seems simple to us now, if not a tad annoying, but at the time it was the height of pleasure. The absolute most fun. Parties, every year as we age, somehow become less and less spontaneous. Like there's some sort of sliding scale we're sliding down each year as we head closer to "maturity" and away from fun.

It doesn't have to be that way. Do things as a hostess to shake your friends up a bit. Get them laughing. Scare them a bit. Woo them with beauty. Thrill them with adventure. Whatever works. But try to get them out of their rut, the "party face" too many of us put on too often. Having a beautiful, carefully trained service staff on hand like we did at this pool party always helps, of course. Old Ambrose certainly took relish in the unexpected, perhaps to a fault, but the spirit with which he wrote is admirable, and we all find that we have to make a little effort to remember to actually enjoy ourselves. So jump in and splash around a bit. It's good for the soul, not to mention the party.

drink
quantities

Assume three drinks per person for every two hours of the party but always have extra on hand.

1 dash = 6 drops

1 pony = 1 ounce

1 jigger = 1½ ounces

1 fifth = 750 milliliters, or 25.6 fluid ounces

1 handle bottle = 1.75 liters, or 55.6 fluid ounces

1 fifth yields anywhere from 12 to 16 drinks

1 750-milliliter bottle of wine yields 6 to 8 glasses

1 case of champagne yields 80 to 100 glasses

party day:
setting up
the bar

What every bar needs, whether it be self-service or tended by a professional:

GLASSES

LIQUORS

MIXERS

ICE (separate tubs for drinks, chilling liquors, and chilling glasses)

SHAKER

JIGGER

STRAINER

BOTTLE OPENER

CORKSCREW

BOWLS OF GARNISHES

CUTTING BOARD AND KNIFE

BAR TOWELS

COCKTAIL NAPKINS

PLACE TO DISCARD ICE

DRINK CARDS (when self-service)

using the
professionals

If you have the budget and want to make it easy on yourself, definitely consider hiring help for the evening. If you are not ready to go all the way with a caterer, try hiring someone to clean up and someone to tend bar.

While you are lighting candles, your cleaning help can tidy the kitchen and plate the last of the hors d'oeuvres and your bartender can prepare the garnishes. During the party, your help will clear and clean dirty glasses and replenish hors d'oeuvres while the bartender keeps everyone in fresh drink. When the party is over, you will have someone to clean up the end of the dishes and break down the bar. Easy.

If this seems too extravagant to you, or if you are having an informal blow-out and don't need all that tending to, try what we do on such occasions—arrange for someone to come by the next morning (make sure they have keys) and clean. If you are lucky, the place will be spotless before you get out of bed.

DRINKS

Key Lime Rickey, 2001

2 ounces gin
1 ounce fresh Key lime juice (see Fresh Fruit
  Juice, page 33)
1 teaspoon simple syrup (recipe on page 23)
Soda water
Key lime slices for garnish

Add the gin, lime juice, simple syrup, and plenty of cracked ice to a shaker, and shake vigorously to combine. Strain into an ice-filled Collins glass and top with the soda water. Add Key lime slices for garnish and serve.

(For photo, see page 61.)

Ruby Slip, 2000

1½ ounces vodka
½ ounce Limoncello
1 ounce fresh raspberry juice (see Fresh Fruit
  Juice, page 33)
1 ounce fresh peach juice
Fresh raspberries and superfine sugar for garnish

Place the vodka, Limoncello, raspberry and peach juices, and plenty of cracked ice in a shaker, and shake vigorously to combine. Strain into a well-chilled cocktail glass. Roll the fresh raspberries in the sugar, garnish the cocktail with a few sugared raspberries, and serve.

Lemongrass Cocktail, 2002

FOR THE COCKTAILS:
1½ ounces vodka
2 ounces Lemongrass Infusion
¼ ounce fresh lemon juice

FOR THE LEMONGRASS INFUSION:
1 cup water
12 inches lemongrass, roughly chopped*
1 tablespoon sugar
*If unavailable at your supermarket, lemongrass can be found at Asian grocers or specialty food stores.

To make the Lemongrass Infusion, combine the water and lemongrass in a saucepan. Bring to boil, then simmer over low heat until reduced by half. Remove from heat, add the sugar, and stir until it dissolves. Cool, then strain, discarding the lemongrass.

Place the vodka, Lemongrass Infusion, lemon juice, and plenty of cracked ice in a shaker, and shake vigorously to combine. Strain into a well-chilled cocktail glass and serve.

East India Cocktail

A scrumptious Prohibition-era drink.

2 ounces brandy
½ ounce curaçao
1½ ounces fresh pineapple juice
1 dash Angostura bitters
Fresh pineapple pieces or orange peel for garnish

Place the brandy, curaçao, pineapple juice, bitters, and plenty of cracked ice in a shaker, and shake vigorously to combine. Strain into a well-chilled cocktail glass, garnish with a small piece of pineapple or a twist of orange, and serve.

FOOD

Vegetarian Spring Rolls with Chili Dipping Sauce

MAKES 16 PIECES PLUS DIPPING SAUCE

FOR THE SPRING ROLLS:
3 ounces mung bean vermicelli*
16 rice paper wrappers*
16 fresh basil leaves
½ cup fresh cilantro
1 cup julienned (cut into matchstick strips) jicama or cucumber
1 cup julienned carrot
1 cup julienned snow peas
1 tablespoon grated lime zest
*Available in Asian markets or specialty food stores

FOR THE DIPPING SAUCE:
⅔ cup water
2 tablespoons sugar
2 tablespoons chili oil
4 tablespoons fish sauce
2 tablespoons white vinegar
1 tablespoon minced fresh red chili pepper
2 tablespoons chopped fresh cilantro

To make the spring rolls, soak the vermicelli in hot water for 10 minutes then drain. Briefly dip a rice paper in lukewarm water until soft, then lay it on a flat surface. In the center of the rice paper, place some vermicelli, 1 basil leaf, 2 teaspoons cilantro, and 1 tablespoon each of jicama, carrot, and snow peas, and a sprinkle of lime zest. Fold two sides over the filling, then roll up the spring roll, starting from one of the open sides. Repeat until you have 16 rolls.

Place the spring rolls, seam side down, on a serving platter and sprinkle with water. Cover with a damp cloth and plastic wrap until serving; the rolls can be made 1 or 2 hours before the party.

To make the dipping sauce, combine the water and sugar in a saucepan over medium heat and stir until the sugar dissolves. Remove from heat and whisk in the chili oil, fish sauce, vinegar, chili pepper, and cilantro; the sauce can be made the night before the party. Serve in small bowls to accompany the spring rolls.

Coconut Chicken and Mango Kebabs

MAKES 16 KEBABS

16 bamboo skewers
2 pounds boneless, skinless chicken breast, cut into 1-inch cubes
2 slightly underripe mangos (about 2 pounds), cut into 1-inch cubes

FOR THE MARINADE:
2 tablespoons chopped shallot
2 cloves garlic, peeled and chopped
2 tablespoons chopped fresh ginger
1 teaspoon ground cumin
1 teaspoon salt
2 tablespoons peanut oil
4 tablespoons unsweetened coconut cream (see Note)
2 tablespoons fresh lime juice

Soak the skewers in water for at least 2 hours—make sure they are completely immersed as they will burn otherwise. In the meantime, prepare the marinade: combine the shallots, garlic, ginger, cumin, salt, oil, coconut cream, and lime juice in a food processor or blender and puree. Place the chicken cubes in a bowl, add the coconut cream puree, and toss to coat. Cover and refrigerate for at least 30 minutes or up to 3 hours. Discard the marinade, reserving the chicken.

Preheat the grill. To assemble the kebabs, thread the chicken and mango cubes onto the skewers, alternating between the two ingredients. Grill over medium heat, about 5 minutes per side or until the chicken is opaque throughout.

NOTE: Unsweetened coconut cream is sold canned or sometimes frozen at Asian markets or specialty food stores. Do not confuse it with cream of coconut, which is sweetened and used primarily for desserts and mixed drinks.

Thai Shrimp Kebabs

MAKES 24 KEBABS

24 bamboo skewers
48 medium shrimp, peeled and deveined (about
1½ pounds)

FOR THE MARINADE:
¾ cup peanut oil
1 tablespoon fish sauce
5 tablespoons grated fresh ginger
1 tablespoon chopped garlic
2 kaffir lime leaves (see Note)
1 small jalapeño pepper, cored, seeded, and
finely chopped
2 tablespoons fresh lime juice
1 tablespoon grated orange zest
1 tablespoon salt

Soak the skewers in water for at least 2 hours—make
sure they are completely immersed as they will burn
otherwise. In the meantime, prepare the marinade,
whisking together the oil, fish sauce, ginger, garlic,
lime leaves, jalapeño, lime juice, orange zest, and
salt in a large bowl. Add the shrimp and toss lightly
to coat. Cover and refrigerate for at least 1 hour or
overnight. Discard the marinade, reserving the
shrimp.

Preheat the grill. Stick two shrimp on one end of
each skewer. Grill until pink, approximately 2 minutes per side. Serve immediately.

NOTE: Used extensively in Thai cooking, kaffir lime
leaves add a wonderful floral-citrus flavor. They are
sold dried, and occasionally fresh, at Asian markets
or specialty food stores. They can be omitted if
they're not available.

cocktails in THE SAND

Eliot's great great-grandfather Alton Hastings

had three daughters and one son. He owned a piece of beachfront property on the end of a point in a sleepy little fishing town in Cape Cod. When it came time to think about passing it on to the next generation, he did something fairly novel: he gave the main house to the son as was customary, but converted the boathouse into a home for one of the daughters and built two smaller (by nineteenth-century standards) houses for the other two.

So Eliot's grandmother grew up summering with all her cousins on the compound. She describes countless afternoon parties that spilled over from house to house, dancing and running around and playing in the water while the adults did a tamer version of the same. The feeling was a remarkable mix of safety and society, because, though they may not all have known each other well, they were family.

A few hurricanes later, the boathouse is still standing, and we like to go from time to time each summer. There is a tremendous sense of timelessness by the seashore. Nothing is better than coming back exhausted from an afternoon of tennis or sailing, or clamming up the bay at low tide—the same activities the family enjoyed a hundred years before—and then gathering for drinks to watch the sunset. We like to invite friends up from New York and dress it up a bit—just for fun—to give the sunset cocktail ritual, and our ancestors without which it wouldn't be possible, the reverence they deserve.

invitations

Printed? Handwritten? Who has time for that anymore? That said, to receive a lovely or playful invite in the actual mail really sets your party apart from others. Be warned, guests will expect a lot more from you when you send an invitation. So wait until you're ready.

Group e-mails (especially using the blind-copying function) are easy and work well. Explore your e-mail program and find a funny background. Some even come with music now. Anything to set yours apart from the drab spam we receive every few minutes.

WHAT TO INCLUDE: Date, location, time, duration, theme, dress or not, and RSVP or not.

ANY EXTRAS: For instance, a map to the location or taxi company phone numbers if it's going to be a late night.

FORMAT: RSVP in the lower left, other essentials in lower right (valet parking, dress requirements, and similar).

Make sure to give your guests adequate time to reply and reserve the space in their calendars. This usually means a little under two weeks; it definitely does not mean two days unless the party is last minute.

Unfortunately, many people have difficulty responding to an invitation even when it is specifically requested. In such cases of shockingly poor behavior, do not hesitate to call the negligent invitee and remind them about the party so you can get a final head count.

ice

Crucial for any party, essential to any drink, there are many kinds of ice, each best for different occasions:

CRACKED: Best for all cocktails, these are irregular shards literally chipped off the block by an ice company. Because of their greater surface area, cracked ice chills drinks at a much faster rate than other options, and when shaken leaves a few of the tiniest remnants to add frost and mystery to a drink.

COCKTAIL: The next best option for the above, these are small, somewhat irregular cubes that are mass-produced.

CRUSHED: Used for blended and a few specialty drinks.

BLOCK: Best for punches and other large drink presentation, or for the supremely ambitious who like to make their own cracked ice.

CUBES: Your generic, chunky ice-tray version, or the harder to find mini-cube tray size. Good for little other than having run out.

FUN ICE PRESENTATION:
Freeze drink garnishes in ice cubes or make ice cubes from a juice used in the cocktail.

For punches, make larger blocks of ice since they will melt slower. Fill a washed milk carton or a mold with water. Add colorful (and always edible) garnishes for color, and freeze.

Always call the wholesale-ice manufacturers directly for both price and delivery ease. This is what caterers do, and every urban area has at least one. They deliver 50-pound bags at extremely reasonable prices. Figure on 1 to 2 pounds per guest for the drinks alone.

the **best** way to quickly **chill**

Immerse the bottle in a tub filled with ice, water, and salt (¼ cup per gallon of water). This will cool wine and beer quickly and delicately.

71

DRINKS

Honeydew Cooler with Watermelon Swizzle, 2002

2 ounces vodka
3 ounces honeydew melon juice (see Note)
½ ounce fresh lemon juice
Sticks of fresh watermelon for garnish

Place vodka, melon juice, lemon juice, and plenty of cracked ice in a shaker and shake vigorously. Strain into a well-chilled cocktail glass and garnish with a watermelon swizzle.

NOTE: If you have trouble making the juice in an electric juicer, peel, seed, and chop a honeydew melon into large chunks and puree the chunks in a blender. Transfer the puree to a wide, shallow bowl and allow it to settle. Scoop off much of the pulp (it will rise to the top), and use the juice that settles at the bottom of the bowl. One medium melon makes about 24 ounces juice.

Plumbed Depths, 2001

2 ounces tequila
2 ounces fresh plum juice (see Fresh Fruit Juice, page 33)
½ ounce simple syrup (recipe on page 23)
Lime wedge for garnish

Place tequila, plum juice, simple syrup, and plenty of cracked ice in a shaker, and shake vigorously to combine. Strain thoroughly into a well-chilled cocktail glass, garnish with a wedge of lime, and serve.

Tropical Champagne Punch

This is a fantastic, light refresher.

SERVES 10

1 bottle champagne
½ cup fresh mango slices
½ cup fresh pineapple chunks
½ cup fresh raspberries
½ cup fresh star fruit slices
1 cup fresh pineapple juice

Place the mango, pineapple chunks, raspberries, star fruit, and plenty of cracked ice in a punch bowl. Add the pineapple juice and pour in the champagne. Serve in water goblets or large wine glasses.

VARIATION: Using ½ cup of the pineapple juice, fill the wells of an ice cube tray half full. In each well, add a chunk of the fruit. Top each cube with water and freeze, then use these flavored ice cubes instead of the cracked ice to keep your punch cool.

Pegu

An old cocktail from the renowned Pegu Club outside Rangoon, Burma.

1½ ounces gin
¾ ounce Cointreau
½ ounce fresh lime juice
Dash Angostura bitters
Lime peel for garnish

Place the gin, Cointreau, lime juice, bitters, and plenty of cracked ice in a shaker, and shake vigorously to combine. Serve in a well-chilled cocktail glass garnished with a lime twist.

FOOD

Smoked Salmon Wheels

MAKES 12 TO 16 LARGE PIECES

1 large cucumber (about ¾ pound)
2 teaspoons salt
4 tablespoons sweet butter, softened
2 tablespoons finely chopped fresh dill
2 teaspoons grated lemon zest
1 loaf good-quality white sandwich bread, unsliced
¼ pound thinly sliced smoked salmon
1 teaspoon fresh lemon juice
½ teaspoon ground white pepper

Peel the cucumber and, using a mandoline or well-trained hand, carefully slice into ¹⁄₁₆-inch-thick slices. Place in a bowl, add the salt, and toss to mix. Let sit for 30 minutes then rinse well, drain, and pat dry with paper towels. Set aside. In another bowl, mix the butter, dill, and lemon zest, and set aside.

Cut the crusts from the loaf, then cut two lengthwise slices, each about 2 inches thick. (These are not slices for sandwiches; you are cutting the loaf the long way.) Using a rolling pin, roll each slice until ½-inch thick. Spread the butter on one side of each slice and arrange slices of cucumber to cover, then layer with salmon slices. Season with the lemon juice and pepper.

To create the wheels, roll up each slice starting from the shorter side, taking care that the ingredients do not fall out as you roll. Wrap the rolls securely in plastic wrap and refrigerate for 2 to 3 hours. When ready to serve, cut each roll into 6 to 8 wheels and arrange on a platter, like sushi.

Asian Lobster Rolls with Dipping Sauce

MAKES 16 PIECES PLUS DIPPING SAUCE

FOR THE DIPPING SAUCE:
1 tablespoon peeled and roughly chopped fresh ginger
2 teaspoons soy sauce
1 tablespoon honey
1 tablespoon rice vinegar
1 teaspoon sesame oil
1 teaspoon salt
¼ teaspoon cayenne pepper
3 tablespoons mayonnaise

FOR THE LOBSTER ROLLS:
1 boiled Maine lobster (about 1½ pounds), picked and chilled
1 European (hothouse) cucumber, peeled (about 1 pound)
16 pickled ginger slices

To make the dipping sauce, puree the ginger, soy sauce, honey, vinegar, oil, salt, and cayenne in a blender. Transfer to a bowl and fold in mayonnaise. The sauce can be made the day before the party and refrigerated in an airtight container; when ready to serve, stir vigorously.

To make the lobster rolls, cut the chilled lobster meat into bite-size pieces. Slice 8 paper-thin pieces of cucumber, lengthwise, using a mandoline or steady hand. Do not use the seeded area, if any. Cut the cucumber slices in half crosswise to create 16 shorter pieces. Lay one cucumber piece flat and add one piece of pickled ginger and a piece of lobster. Roll the cucumber around the lobster, and secure with a toothpick. Repeat until you have 16 rolls; serve with the dipping sauce.

Caviar Cake with Toast Points

SERVES 12

8 eggs, hard-boiled and diced
⅓ cup mayonnaise
1 tablespoon finely chopped fresh parsley
2 tablespoons finely chopped celery
2 teaspoons Dijon mustard
¼ teaspoon salt
½ cup finely chopped red onion
½ cup sour cream
3 ounces inexpensive black caviar, such as
**   black whitefish roe**
1 ounce inexpensive red caviar, such as salmon roe

Toast points or crackers

Combine the eggs, mayonnaise, parsley, celery, mustard, and salt to create egg salad. On a large serving plate, neatly spread the egg salad in a circle. Sprinkle the red onion on top, then spread a layer of the sour cream, followed by a layer of the black caviar. Decorate with the red caviar to finish the caviar cake. Serve immediately with the toast points. (For photo of Caviar Cake served on a platter, see page 3.)

CROQUET party

Alexandra's uncle George Herrick is one of the world's experts on croquet, not so much on the sport or gamesmanship, but on its history. It's an interesting area of expertise, as the origins of the game are still shrouded in mystery. There is some speculation that croquet and all bat and ball games descend from a fertility ritual performed by the pharoahs of ancient Egypt. But little is known of its history from then on until it became a fashionable pastime in England in 1850. It is hardly a coincidence that the lawn mower was invented about the same time, which made the game much more playable and enticing.

He writes about the rise of the game in America. "It was at Nahant, on that small island in Boston harbor where one of the first summer resorts sprang up, that Frederick Tudor staked out in 1859 the first American croquet lawn that we know." Within a few years, croquet had taken off like wildfire. There were suddenly croquet clubs in fashionable resort areas and many of the estates up and down the eastern seaboard had lawns installed to match Tudor's.

Croquet parties were all the rage throughout the 1860s and 70s, before tennis took over as the sport of the moment. Guests would dress in the all-white outfits we still know today (though at the time this was dressing down, their version of athletic apparel), and come together in the late afternoon for games, snacks, and refreshing beverages. For a while, before the fashion vanished quickly and mysteriously, croquet parties were both de rigueur and an enormous amount of fun.

It is sometimes delightful to have an event at a party, and we know of no better event for a summer evening than a good round of croquet. Its leisurely pace provides ample time for drinking and conversing. In fact, we tend to have games that last till well after sunset—certain players always get carried away by ribald jokes and stories. It's a lovely way to spend an evening: outside in the fresh air, with fabulous summer drinks and rounds of tasty canapés to complement them.

we got game

There comes a time in the life of any party—or in the span of any friendship—when conversation is better replaced by activity. When all the guests know each other too well and have nothing to say, when the guests are all complete strangers and feel too stiff to speak comfortably, or when they speak comfortably but the mix is such that an uncomfortable political debate is inevitable, then play a game. Games are not for everybody, and are certainly not for every party, but they can be a terrific, fun way to liven up a group and get their juices flowing.

a drink by any other name . . .

Phrases through the ages for man's favorite pastime:

Whet your whistle (the oldest known,

   from Chaucer's *Canterbury Tales,* 1386)

Bend your elbow

Breathe a prayer

Fire a slug

Give a Chinaman a music lesson

Go see the dog about a man

Hang one on

Kiss the book

Name it

Shave the guts

Shed a tear

Slop down

Sluice your bold

Soak your chaffer

Sugar the kidney

Tank up

Tap the admiral

Up the bucket

Wet the sickle

on the rocks versus straight up

Most of the cocktail recipes that we offer in this book are designed to be served straight up. This is not to mean that this is the only way to enjoy these drinks. If you or your guests prefer a slightly weaker drink or are longing for loads of ice on a hot summer day, feel free to serve them on the rocks. The recipe in such cases will be exactly the same; after mixing, just strain the drink into an ice-filled tumbler or Collins glass.

DRINKS

Sheets to the Wind, 2000

1 ounce brandy
1 ounce Lillet Blanc
1 ounce Limoncello
1 ounce fresh blueberry juice (see Fresh Fruit
**   Juice, page 33)**
1 ounce fresh lemon juice
Lemon wheel for garnish

Place the brandy, Lillet, Limoncello, blueberry juice, lemon juice, and plenty of cracked ice in a shaker, and shake vigorously to combine. Strain thoroughly into a well-chilled cocktail glass, garnish with a lemon wheel, and serve.

Southampton, 2001

2 ounces vodka
2 sprigs fresh mint, plus more for garnish
1 ounce fresh lime juice
½ ounce simple syrup (recipe on page 23)

Place the mint in a shaker and muddle until oils are released. Add the vodka, lime juice, simple syrup, and plenty of cracked ice, and shake vigorously to combine. Strain into an ice-filled old-fashioned glass, garnish with a mint sprig, and serve.
(For photo, see page 81.)

Eve's Tryst, 2002

1½ ounces gin
½ ounce Campari
¼ ounce Cointreau
2 ounces fresh ruby red grapefruit juice
¼ ounce fresh lemon juice
Orange peel to garnish

Place the gin, Campari, Cointreau, grapefruit juice, lemon juice, and plenty of cracked ice in a shaker, and shake vigorously to combine. Strain thoroughly into an ice-filled tumbler, and garnish with the orange twist.

FOOD

Minted Shrimp Canapés on a Bed of Pea and Sorrel Puree

MAKES 20 PIECES

FOR THE TOASTS:

10 pieces thinly sliced (¼- to ⅓-inch-thick) white bread
1 tablespoon light olive oil

FOR THE PUREE:

2 tablespoons sweet butter
1 medium clove garlic, minced
3 medium shallots, finely chopped
1 tablespoon water
¾ cup peas, fresh or frozen (thawed)
½ cup fresh sorrel
1 teaspoon salt or to taste

FOR THE SHRIMP:

10 medium shrimp, unpeeled
2 cups water
¾ cup salt
1 tablespoon sweet butter
2 tablespoons finely chopped fresh mint
½ teaspoon finely ground red pepper plus additional to taste

Heat the broiler. To make the toasts, cut twenty small circles from the slices of bread using a juice glass or cookie cutter. (You should be able to cut two rounds from each slice.) Brush both sides of the bread very lightly with the oil. Broil on a baking sheet until golden brown, about 1 minute per side. Watch carefully since thin toast burns easily. If refrigerated in an airtight container, the toasts can be prepared up to 4 days in advance of serving. Otherwise, set aside.

To make the puree, melt the butter in a saucepan over low heat, add the garlic and shallots, and cook 6 to 8 minutes or until soft. Add the water and peas, gently stirring to combine, and continue cooking 2 to 3 minutes until the peas are slightly tender. Combine the pea mixture, sorrel, and salt in a food processor or blender, and puree until smooth. Adjust salt to taste. This puree can be made a day in advance if refrigerated in an airtight container. If serving immediately, set aside to cool to room temperature.

To prepare the shrimp, brine by soaking in the water and ¾ cup salt for 20 minutes, then peel and devein the shrimp. Melt the butter in a skillet over high heat. When the butter begins to bubble, toss in the shrimp and cook for 2 minutes. Reduce heat, turn over the shrimp, and cook until pink, 1 to 2 minutes longer; be careful not to overcook. Remove from heat and add the mint and pepper, tossing to combine.

To assemble, bring the pea and sorrel puree to room temperature, if refrigerated. Slice the shrimp in half, lengthwise. Spread about 2 teaspoons puree on each toast, place half a shrimp on top, and sprinkle lightly with red pepper, if desired.

Sesame-Encrusted Rice Balls with Smoked Salmon and Wasabi Dipping Sauce

MAKES 16 PIECES PLUS DIPPING SAUCE

FOR THE RICE BALLS:

2 cups short-grain white rice

2 cups less 2 tablespoons water

1½ tablespoons rice vinegar

½ teaspoon sugar

½ teaspoon salt

½ cup sesame seeds (black seeds are the most dramatic)

¼ pound smoked salmon, finely chopped

1 tablespoon minced capers

½ teaspoon grated lemon zest

FOR THE DIPPING SAUCE:

¼ cup soy sauce

2 tablespoons water

¼ teaspoon wasabi paste*

*Available at Asian grocers or specialty food stores

To make the rice balls, wash and thoroughly rinse the rice. Place the water and rice in a heavy pot and soak for 30 minutes. Cover, bring to a boil over high heat, then immediately reduce heat to low. Cook for 15 minutes or until water has completely evaporated. Transfer to a bowl and set aside. Combine the rice vinegar, sugar, and salt in a small glass. Pour the vinegar mixture into the rice, stirring to combine, but be careful not to crush the rice grains. Place a damp towel over the rice and set aside to cool.

Toast the sesame seeds in a heavy nonstick skillet over low heat, stirring constantly, until their scent is released; spread on a plate to cool. Combine the smoked salmon, capers, and lemon zest in a bowl and set aside.

When ready to assemble, fill a bowl with warm water. Dip your hands in the water and dry lightly on a damp towel. Take approximately 1 tablespoon rice in one hand and flatten it. With the other hand, take about ½ teaspoon salmon mixture and place in the center of the rice. Take another tablespoon of rice and place on top of the salmon, and roll to create a ball. Roll the rice ball in the toasted sesame seeds, and place on a serving platter. Rinse hands in water, drying lightly, and repeat until you've made all 16.

To make the dipping sauce, combine the soy sauce, water, and wasabi in a small bowl and mix well. Serve as an accompaniment to the rice balls. The sauce can be made the night before, but the rice balls should be made only 1 to 2 hours before serving.

Cucumber Cups with Sweet Pepper Coulis

MAKES ABOUT 24 PIECES

1 large red bell pepper
1 medium yellow bell pepper
2 small red chili peppers
1 medium tomato
¼ cup extra-virgin olive oil
1 teaspoon salt
1 teaspoon finely chopped fresh thyme
4 Japanese or European (hothouse) cucumbers
(about 3½ pounds)

Preheat the broiler. Cut the peppers in half lengthwise, discarding seeds and membranes. Place the pepper halves, skin side up, on a foil-lined baking sheet; flatten with your hand. Broil 3 inches from heat for 12 minutes or until skin has blackened. Place in a paper bag; seal and let stand for at least 15 minutes. When cool, remove from the bag, discard the skins, chop, and set aside.

Using a paring knife, strike an X in one end of the tomato. Bring a saucepan of water to boil and immerse the tomato for 30 seconds. Remove, and when cool enough to handle, peel, core, and mince. Combine the pepper, tomato, oil, salt, and thyme to make the coulis. The recipe can be prepared to this point up to 2 days before the party; refrigerate in an airtight container.

If the cucumbers are waxed, it is necessary to peel them. If not, leave the skins on or make decorative stripes using a peeler. Cut each cucumber into a minimum of 6 slices, each about 1¼-inches thick.

Using a melon baller, scoop out the centers of each slice to create cups to hold the coulis. Cover the cups with a slightly damp towel and refrigerate for up to 4 hours.

When you're ready to assemble, fill the cucumber cups with the coulis. Serve chilled or at room temperature.

RENDEZVOUS
à deux

In the vast tome that is _Anna Karenina,_ we
are introduced to hundreds of characters, all with far too many names, but one couple stands out. They are only mentioned briefly, a beautiful, older couple who are the best dancers at a famous ball. What the narrator knew them for, it seems, was their habit of rarely speaking to each other and always dancing with attractive young partners. In the midst of this enormous, glamorous party, their eyes barely met, but the connection between them was intense. It was palpable. You could sense it across the room. They seemed to like it this way—to thrive on the energy. And they always left together.

Attraction. Aqua Vitae was hired recently to design a party for two, the ultimate date. Our hostess wanted to stage an elegant seduction, surrounding her gentleman caller in luxury and grace. We reconfigured her living room to create a few boudoiresque touches—covered the couches with silks, floated gardenias in silver bowls, and dotted the room with hundreds of votives—and hired a beautiful staff to serve the pair extravagantly tasteful cocktails and canapés. It became quite clear quite quickly that the lady of the house was having her every desire met, so much so that our bartender was summarily dismissed. We still consider it one of our greatest events. It is in her honor, and for the irrepressible romantic in all of us, that we created this chapter.

entering the **atmosphere**

When thinking about atmosphere, consider appealing to all of the senses:

VISUAL: through lighting, flowers, fabrics, glassware

TACTILE: through fabrics and linens

OLFACTORY: through flowers, food, and scented candles

AURAL: through music and cocktail shaking

TASTE: through cocktails and hors d'oeuvres

the **right light**

- Dim all the lights and turn down or even turn off those bright overheads.

- Use candles to make the room and the guests glow—drab becomes fabulous in their amber haze.

- Be careful, however, not to make it too dark. A total shortage of light nips the energy from the room and creates an ambiance reminiscent of a séance.

- Don't forget to light the entrance (the outside entrance, too, if you can). This sets the tone for the party as the guests arrive. Lanterns work wonderfully and are available in many colors and styles at reasonable cost.

- If you don't have enough candlesticks, use your imagination. Try clusters of tea candles on little plates, fill vases with pebbles to secure the candlesticks, or fill clear glass bowls with water and floating candles.

- To slow the burn, cool candles in the refrigerator for a few hours before the party begins.

DRINKS

Aviation

Although this is one of the absolute best old-school drinks, it is almost never served. Sip this and lose your fear of flying.

1½ ounce gin
¾ ounce maraschino liqueur
¾ ounce fresh lemon juice
Maraschino cherry for garnish

Place all ingredients except the cherry garnish in a shaker, along with plenty of cracked ice, and shake vigorously to combine. Strain into a well-chilled cocktail glass and garnish with the maraschino cherry.

Alberto's Cocktail

Our version of the standard created by the drink master at La Caravelle in New York City.

1½ ounces vodka
3 ounces champagne
3 fresh mint sprigs
1 ounce fresh lime juice
½ ounce simple syrup (recipe on page 23)

Place the mint sprigs in a shaker and muddle until oils are released. Add the vodka, lime juice, simple syrup, and plenty of cracked ice, and shake vigorously to combine, then strain into a water goblet or wine glass. Top with the champagne and serve.

VARIATION: If you want to create a truly awe-inspiring drink, make this with mint–infused simple syrup.

Damsel's Leap, 1999

1½ ounces light rum
¾ ounce fresh lime juice
¾ ounce fresh grapefruit juice
1 teaspoon grenadine
Fresh cherry (with stem) for garnish

Place the rum, lime juice, grapefruit juice, and grenadine in a shaker, along with plenty of cracked ice, and shake vigorously to combine. Strain into a well-chilled cocktail glass, garnish with the cherry, and serve.

De Rigueur Cocktail

This inspired but almost-forgotten Jazz Age treasure is something to share with your honey.

2 ounces whiskey
1 ounce fresh grapefruit juice
1 ounce honey

Place all the ingredients, along with plenty of cracked ice, in a shaker, and shake vigorously to combine. Strain into a well-chilled cocktail glass and serve.

FOOD

Cheese Crisps with White Bean Puree

Strong in flavor and incredibly easy to make, these chips are our interpretation of those popular in Italian wine bars. They are the prefect complement to a mellow dip, such as our White Bean Puree. The dip calls for raw garlic but—have no fear—if both of you are eating it, you will smell fantastic to each other! And don't forget garlic's supposed aphrodisiac qualities.

MAKES 6 CRISPS PLUS 1 CUP DIP

FOR THE CRISPS:
½ cup grated Parmigiano-Reggiano (do not use a processed, pregrated Parmesan)
½ cup grated Asiago cheese
1 teaspoon olive oil

FOR THE DIP:
1 cup cooked cannellini beans
2 tablespoons olive oil
1 teaspoon minced garlic
1 teaspoon fresh lemon juice
Salt and pepper to taste

To make the crisps, preheat the oven to 350°F (see Note). Combine the cheeses in a bowl. Line a baking sheet with parchment paper and rub lightly with the olive oil. Sprinkle the cheese mix onto the parchment in desired shapes—we prefer strips approximately 1½ inches by 3 inches. Bake until lightly browned, about 8 minutes. Transfer the crisps to paper towels to drain any excess oil, and serve the day they are prepared.

To make the dip, place the beans, olive oil, garlic, and lemon juice in a food processor, and process to form a thick puree. Add salt and pepper to taste, process again, and refrigerate for 2 to 3 hours or serve immediately.

VARIATION: If you are a fan of anchovies, omit the salt from the puree and instead season with 1 teaspoon anchovy paste and 1 tablespoon finely chopped fresh parsley. Process and serve.

NOTE: If no oven is available, the crisps can be pan-fried in a nonstick skillet over high heat.

Polenta *Crostini* with Wild Mushrooms and Prosciutto

MAKES 8 PIECES

FOR THE *CROSTINI*:

½ cup polenta

2 cups water

1 teaspoon salt

2 tablespoons sweet butter

Olive oil

FOR THE MUSHROOMS AND PROSCUITTO:

3 tablespoons olive oil

1 teaspoon minced garlic

2 cups chopped wild mushrooms (we use a
mixture of portabello and cremini mushrooms)

½ teaspoon salt

½ teaspoon black pepper

1 tablespoon fresh parsley

2 teaspoons white wine

¼ cup shredded prosciutto

To make the *crostini*, combine the polenta and water in a saucepan over medium heat. Bring to a soft boil, stirring often to prevent the polenta from clumping. Reduce the heat to low, and simmer until the polenta is no longer grainy and quite thick, 20 to 25 minutes. Remove from heat, add the salt and butter, and mix thoroughly.

Pour the polenta onto a lightly greased baking sheet, and spread it with a spoon until about ½-inch thick. Refrigerate for 1 hour or until firm, then cut into decorative shapes using cookie cutters or a paring knife. Preheat the broiler to high. (If you do not have a broiler, you can bake the crisps in your oven at 400°F.) Lightly brush both sides of the polenta pieces with olive oil, place on a nonstick baking sheet, and broil until golden brown, about 3 minutes. Turn over and continue broiling until crisp, about 2 minutes. Set aside to cool.

To make the mushroom-proscuitto mixture, heat the olive oil in a sauté pan over medium heat. Add the garlic and sauté for 2 minutes, until soft. Add the mushrooms, salt, pepper, and parsley and continue to cook, stirring frequently, for about 5 minutes. Add the wine, turn the heat to high, and cook for 30 seconds more, then remove from heat. Stir in the prosciutto.

To assemble, place 1 to 2 tablespoons of the mushroom-proscuitto mixture (or as much as you can comfortably fit) on top of each *crostini*. Serve these hors d'oeuvres fresh and warm.

(For photo, see page 8.)

Roasted Cherry Tomatoes with Ricotta and Fresh Sage

This wonderful appetizer shows that there's more than one way to stuff a cherry tomato. We provide a recipe for a simple ricotta stuffing here, but other things to try include a smoked trout or salt cod puree, goat cheese and roasted pepper, or—for a vegan's delight—a spoonful of ratatouille.

MAKES 8 PIECES

8 cherry tomatoes
⅓ cup whole-milk ricotta cheese
1 teaspoon finely chopped fresh sage
½ teaspoon salt
Pinch of black pepper

Preheat the oven to 350°F. Cut off the tops of the tomatoes and, using a small paring knife or melon baller, remove the seeds. (Be careful not to pierce the bottoms of the tomatoes.)

In a small bowl, combine the ricotta, sage, salt, and pepper. Using a small spoon, fill each tomato to the brim with the ricotta mixture. Place the stuffed tomatoes on a nonstick baking sheet and bake for 8 minutes or until warmed through. Be careful not to bake too long or the tomatoes will be too hot to handle. Serve warm.

(For photo, see page 8.)

GARAGE
mixer

Some of the most beautiful and interesting
theater in the world is site specific. That is, theatrical productions that are tailored to, and sometimes written for, a certain space—often a nontraditional one. There are theatrical companies
that specialize in site-specific theater, and do it incredibly well: En Garde Arts in New York,
Theatre de Soleil in Paris, and De La Guarda in Argentina come to mind. These companies take
spaces that we have never thought theatrical—the steps of a Wall Street museum, the interior
of a Masonic Hall, an old shipping pier along a river—and turn them into something glorious and
thought-provoking.

We bring up this up only because all parties are, fundamentally, theater. The host is the director-
producer and the guests are both cast and audience, or either, depending on their inclination.
We once staged a party in a townhouse where every room was an entirely different experience.
One room featured a grand piano and cocktail tables. The next had go-go dancers on platforms.
There was a room filled floor to ceiling with balloons, and another lined entirely with pillows with
a baby pool full of expensive champagne and four-foot straws at its center.

The host of a party should transform the space into something beautiful and vibrant—whether
it is a townhouse or, as in this case, a garage—and let the drama unfold. We think parties in an
unexpected space, such as a garage or the basement of an apartment building, to be lots of fun
and a terrific solution to not having a great amount of personal entertaining space. So bring in
your set designers, and prepare for the players to walk the boards.

planning ahead: **the cooking**

- Always serve some food. It is required if you are drinking, and it keeps nervous hands busy.

- Plan your menu based on the time, your ability, and season.

- Do not include too many recipes on your menu that require last-minute preparation.

- Reviewing menus and charting your course far in advance really helps if there are time constraints.

- Make sure you have all the required cooking utensils and adequate space for food preparation.

- Every hors d'oeuvre should take one bite to eat (or maybe two, if the item is not flaky).

- If you're setting up a large buffet, pull the table from the wall to allow guests to circulate around it.

- Know that people eat more when they serve themselves.

transforming a space

Almost any space can house a great party. You just have to find a way to make it both comfortable and interesting. We often drape painter's canvasses over unsightly walls and furniture. Or, as we did here, go to Chinatown for lively paper lanterns and an Indian store for colorful saris and fabrics.

If your party space is a garage, pull the car out into the driveway, line the trunk with plastic, and turn it into the bar. Then push everything in the garage to the sides, line with canvasses, and bring in a few choice pieces of furniture. In half an hour, you've created a space that looks fabulous and where you can party as hard as you want to.

DRINKS

Ginger Sunset, 2001

This is the perfect cocktail for a clear fall evening. The ginger adds a slight bite to the sweet pear juice. A wonderful variation is to replace the pear juice with apricot juice as we have done for this party.

2 ounces vodka
2 teaspoons grated fresh ginger
2 ounces fresh pear juice (see Fresh Fruit Juice, page 33)
½ ounce fresh lemon juice
Fresh ginger, peeled and thinly sliced, for garnish

To extract the juice from the grated ginger, press through a cheesecloth into a shaker. Add the vodka, pear juice, lemon juice, and plenty of cracked ice to the shaker, and shake vigorously to combine. Strain thoroughly into a well-chilled cocktail glass, garnish with a ginger slice, and serve.

(Pear Ginger Sunset is pictured on page 16.)

Orchard's Bloom, 2000

1½ ounces vodka
½ ounce Calvados
2 ounces Granny Smith or other tart apple juice (see Fresh Fruit Juice, page 33)
1 teaspoon simple syrup (recipe on page 23)
Dash of fresh lemon juice
Apple slice for garnish

Place vodka, Calvados, apple juice, simple syrup, lemon juice, and plenty of cracked ice in a shaker, and shake vigorously to combine. Strain thoroughly into a well-chilled cocktail glass, garnish with the apple slice, and serve.

Bar Harbor, 2001

It is very important not to use processed cranberry juice in this recipe—it is too sweet and will alter the flavor of the drink dramatically. Buy unprocessed juice in the natural foods section of the supermarket or make our homemade version below.

FOR THE COCKTAILS:
1½ ounces brandy
½ ounce Limoncello
1½ ounces fresh cranberry juice or Homemade Cranberry Juice
Fresh cranberries for garnish

FOR THE HOMEMADE CRANBERRY JUICE:
1 cup fresh or unsweetened frozen cranberries
1 cup water
½ cup sugar or more to taste

To make the Homemade Cranberry Juice, add the cranberries and water to a saucepan and bring to boil. Lower the heat and simmer uncovered for about 15 minutes, or until the berries have just begun to pop. Add the sugar (remember that the Limoncello will add extra sweetness to the drink), stirring until the sugar dissolves. Remove from heat to cool, then strain, reserving the berries for the garnish.

Place the brandy, Limoncello, cranberry juice, and plenty of cracked ice in a shaker, and shake vigorously to combine. Strain thoroughly into a well-chilled cocktail glass, garnish with the fresh cranberries, and serve.

FOOD

Bliss Potatoes with Caviar and Crème Fraîche

MAKES 25 PIECES

25 1½-inch-long new potatoes (or the smallest you can find)
1 teaspoon plus 1 tablespoon salt
⅓ cup good-quality olive oil
½ cup crème fraîche
4 ounces black caviar
25 sprigs fresh dill

Place the potatoes and 1 teaspoon salt in a saucepan and add cold water to cover. Bring to a boil over high heat, reduce to a simmer, and cook until the potatoes are just tender, 10 to 15 minutes, but not so long that the skins split. Remove from heat, drain, and set aside to cool. If you are preparing in advance, the potatoes may be refrigerated at this point in an airtight container for up to one day.

Preheat the oven to 425°F. Trim the ends off the potatoes, and if you have larger potatoes, you may want to cut them in half. With a small melon baller or tiny spoon, scoop out a teaspoon or so of flesh and discard or reserve for another use. Place the potatoes in a large mixing bowl and add the oil and remaining salt. Toss very gently to coat. Place on a nonstick baking sheet, and bake for 10 to 15 minutes or until quite tender and slightly browned. Cool slightly so the crème fraîche won't melt.

Spoon one teaspoon crème fraîche into each potato, and top with the caviar and a sprig of fresh dill. Serve slightly warm or at room temperature.

Roasted Cremini Mushrooms with Walnut–Basil Pesto

MAKES 20 PIECES

FOR THE PESTO:
¾ cup fresh basil leaves
1 large (or 2 small) garlic cloves, minced
⅓ cup chopped walnuts
⅓ cup extra-virgin olive oil
⅓ cup grated Parmigiano cheese
1 tablespoon grated Romano cheese
1 teaspoon salt

FOR THE MUSHROOMS:
20 small cremini mushrooms (about 12 ounces)
1 tablespoon sweet butter
¼ teaspoon salt
¼ cup fine dry breadcrumbs
1 tablespoon extra-virgin olive oil

Preheat the oven to 400°F.

To make the pesto, combine the basil, garlic, walnuts, olive oil, cheeses, and salt in a food processor, and process until creamy. Set aside. The pesto can be made the night before the party and refrigerated.

To make the mushrooms, first clean and destem them. Set aside the caps and finely chop the stems. Melt the butter in a sauté pan over medium heat, then sauté the mushroom stems until soft, about 3 to 4 minutes. Add the salt and breadcrumbs, tossing to combine, then transfer to a mixing bowl. When the mushroom mixture has cooled, add the pesto and stir to combine.

Brush the top and bottom of each mushroom cap with oil. Place on a baking sheet with cap sides up, and roast for 8 to 10 minutes or until liquid begins to seep from the mushrooms. Turn the mushrooms over, fill each with 1 to 2 teaspoons pesto mixture, and serve hot.

Mini Dill Burger *Crostini* with Hot Pepper Spread

MAKES 20 PIECES

FOR THE *CROSTINI*:
1 loaf thinly sliced white bread
4 tablespoons sweet butter

FOR THE SPREAD:
2 teaspoons sweet butter
1 tablespoon fresh lemon juice
1 tablespoon Worcestershire sauce
½ teaspoon Tabasco
Freshly ground pepper to taste

FOR THE BURGERS:
1 pound hamburger
2 tablespoons chopped fresh dill
Salt to taste
¼ pound Havarti cheese, thinly sliced

Ketchup or mustard to top (optional)

Preheat the broiler. With a 2-inch cookie cutter or another desired shape, cut out 20 miniature hamburger buns (the *crostini*), both tops and bottoms. Lightly butter each slice. Place on a baking sheet, and broil for 1 minute or until the slices begin to toast. Flip the slices and continue to toast for another minute. Be careful to avoid burning them—this happens faster than you'd think. The *crostini* buns can be toasted ahead of time and stored for a day or two in an airtight container.

To make the spread, combine the butter, lemon juice, Worcestershire sauce, Tabasco, and pepper to taste in a saucepan, and warm over low heat until the butter melts. Stir and set aside to cool. The spread can be made the night before the party.

In medium bowl, combine the hamburger and dill, mixing thoroughly, and roll into twenty 1-inch balls. Sprinkle a heavy nonstick skillet with salt to taste, and place over medium heat for 5 minutes. Add the hamburger balls to the skillet and sear the meat on one side, 1½ to 2 minutes. Turn the balls over and flatten to ½-inch-thick burgers, then sear the other side. Lower the heat and place a slice of cheese on top of each burger. Cook until done to your liking.

To assemble, put some spread on the bottom half of each bun and on top of that place one burger. Add a dollop of ketchup or mustard on each, if desired, then the top halves of the buns. Serve immediately.
(For photo, see page 104.)

local

BAR

bash

The cocktail is a fundamentally American invention.

The first-known reference to cocktails appeared in 1806 in a New York City newspaper, and cocktails were sampled all over the United States throughout the nineteenth century. But it was not until the "Noble Experiment" of 1920, what came quickly to be known as Prohibition by unhappy tipplers from all walks of life, that the cocktail went from an aficionado's delight to a wildly popular drink in just a few years.

The moment drinking was abolished, seemingly everybody drank. Suddenly, cocktails were everywhere. And the way we drank them changed as well because drinking took place primarily in private, and women were allowed to be seen drinking with men for the first time. As the environment shifted from the all-male saloon to the much more elegant speakeasy, to please the women, impeccable design and formal dress became de rigueur, and drinking became a celebration.

But the American saloon, the ubiquitous corner bar, still has a place in all of our hearts. Instead of the latest overcrowded and ultratrendy *boîte,* what better place to have a birthday party than your local bar. It's loaded with charm, or at least with old regulars, and you can often have it mostly to yourselves. The design is often so simple it's easy to spruce up. Bring the world's two greatest creations—the cocktail and women—into the dusky saloon, and we have a delicious mix indeed.

picking
the day

The night of the week is a big choice, and will often reflect the tone of the party. On Saturday night, people will be at their most relaxed and stay the latest. This is best for the biggest parties or lively groups. Thursday is also really good since it has become generally accepted as a late, almost-end-of-the-week night. Friday is actually difficult. We find people tend to be low energy, exhausted both from the week and Thursday's excesses. It's good for a low-key dinner or gathering.

There's a set of people that swears by Monday night for socializing because they believe it attracts the fewest number of hangers-on, so you may be surprised how lively a Monday night can get. Be warned: Our friend Audrey started a regular Monday evening party at a popular French restaurant in Hollywood, with the idea it would have a closed guest list. And it quickly became too crowded even to get to the men's room, let alone the bar.

making a **schedule**

This is an unfortunate necessity in no matter what locale you are hosting. Even a simple party at your local watering hole requires some planning. Everyone has his or her own checklist, the important thing is just to have one. If you don't, follow our general guidelines below and tailor them to your event.

In the concept phase, you should set:

Date

Time

Occasion/theme

Guest list

Budget

Menu

Location

Music

Next break your list into a schedule:

WEEK OF PARTY: Buy everything that is not perishable. Check your glassware and linens and any service items. Confirm information with the bartender, caterer, or rental company, if you are hiring their services. Order ice delivery. Know your RSVP list. Clean out your refrigerator.

DAY BEFORE PARTY: Purchase perishables. Prepare any foods and juices that can be made in advance. Clean the house. Organize the music. Test cocktails. Arrange flowers or decorations.

DAY OF PARTY: Set up the space. Finish all cocktail and food preparation. Arrange the food on platters and fill pitchers with the mixers.

LAST MINUTE: Bring out the hors d'oeuvres and fill the ice buckets. Light all the candles, turn down the overheads, put on some music, and have a drink.

sprucing up
the local

A bar is a great place to throw a party. You don't have to hire a staff, there's no clean up, and if you choose not to cover the tab, you don't have to spend a lot of money and can still have fun with your friends. To do so, though, here are a few ideas to help make your local bar more personal:

● **Talk to the manager about lighting. If you are allowed to burn candles, bring lots of votives, and turn down the overheads.**

● **Decorate individual tables with flowers and linens.**

● **If the bar has a stereo, bring your own CDs, or some bars will let you hire a dj.**

● **Bring food and set it up on a single table covered with a linen cloth, or place munchies in small bowls around the bar.**

● **Talk to the bartender a week beforehand about any special drinks you may want to serve. Put up frames with a description of each drink for guests to choose from.**

DRINKS

Although every bartender may not be familiar with the following classics, we chose these drinks because all of the ingredients should be readily available at any corner bar.

Old-Fashioned

2 ounces whiskey
1 lump sugar
2 dashes Angostura bitters
1 orange wheel
Soda water
Maraschino cherry for garnish

In an old-fashioned glass, muddle the sugar, bitters, and orange wheel. Fill the glass with ice, top with the whiskey, and stir. Garnish with the maraschino cherry and serve.

Sidecar

First mixed in Paris at the height of World War I (or so the story goes), this delicious concoction pays tribute to the motorcycle's sidecar, the preferred mode of transport for officers at the time.

2 ounces brandy
1 ounce Cointreau
1 ounce fresh lemon juice
Lemon wheel and bar sugar for garnish

Place the brandy, Cointreau, lemon juice, and plenty of cracked ice in a shaker, and shake vigorously to combine. Strain thoroughly into a well-chilled cocktail glass or a snifter. Dip the lemon wheel in the sugar for the garnish and serve.

Gimlet

This drink was reportedly invented by the sailors of the British Royal Navy because both the gin and the lime were believed to fend off scurvy. Perhaps more importantly, gimlets would have made the long, hard days at sea more tolerable.

2 ounces gin
2 ounces Rose's lime juice
Lime wedge for garnish

Place the gin, lime juice, and plenty of cracked ice in a shaker, and shake vigorously to combine. Strain thoroughly into a well-chilled cocktail glass, garnish with the lime wedge, and serve.

Bling Bling, 2001

1½ ounces tequila
1½ ounces fresh grapefruit juice
Ginger ale
Lime wedge for garnish

Place tequila, grapefruit juice, and plenty of cracked ice in a shaker, and shake vigorously to combine. Strain thoroughly into an old-fashioned glass filled with ice, and top with ginger ale. Squeeze the lime wedge over the drink, toss it in, and serve.

Fine and Dandy

This is a classic but rarely served 1920s libation.

2 ounces gin
1 ounce Cointreau
1 ounce fresh lemon juice
1 dash Angostura bitters

Place all the ingredients in a shaker with plenty of cracked ice, and shake vigorously to combine. Strain into a well-chilled cocktail glass and serve.

FOOD

Bar Nuts

You can use almost any mixture of nuts, but we like the following combination. Be sure to use raw, unsalted nuts.

MAKES 6 CUPS NUTS

1½ cups walnuts
1½ cups almonds
1½ cups cashews
1½ cups hazelnuts
2 tablespoons sweet butter
2 tablespoons brown sugar
1 tablespoon maple syrup
2 teaspoons cayenne pepper
2 teaspoons paprika
1 tablespoon fresh lime juice
2 tablespoons kosher salt

Preheat the oven to 350°F. Place the nuts on a baking sheet and toast until golden brown, 15 to 20 minutes. Transfer to a mixing bowl and set aside. In a small saucepan, melt butter over low heat. Stir in the sugar and maple syrup until dissolved, remove from heat, then add the cayenne, paprika, lime juice, and salt and stir. Pour over the nuts and toss to mix. These nuts can be stored in an airtight container for 1 or 2 weeks before serving.

Potato Chips with Tomato-and-Mint Salsa

We prefer the less acidic yellow tomatoes for this salsa, but ripe red ones are almost as good.

MAKES 3 CUPS SALSA AND ONE
GOOD-SIZE BOWL CHIPS

FOR THE CHIPS:
5 large baking potatoes (about 4 pounds)
5 tablespoons vegetable oil
4 tablespoons salt
2 tablespoons crushed pink peppercorns

FOR THE SALSA:
5 large ripe tomatoes (about 2½ pounds)
¾ cup minced vidalia onion
¼ cup chopped fresh mint
2 tablespoons balsamic vinegar
2 tablespoons olive oil
1 teaspoon salt

Preheat the oven to 325°F. To make the chips, wash the unpeeled potatoes thoroughly and slice into thin (about 1/16-inch thick) slices using a mandoline. Place the slices in a large bowl and toss with the oil and salt. Arrange as many slices as you can fit on a nonstick baking sheet (you will have to make several batches), and sprinkle with the pepper. Bake the chips for 10 minutes, then flip and bake for another 5 minutes or until golden brown. Transfer the chips to a plate lined with paper towels and cool completely. Repeat with the remaining potato slices. The chips will stay crisp for up to one week if cooled completely then stored in an airtight container.

To make the salsa, strike an X in one end of each tomato using a paring knife. Bring a saucepan of water to boil and immerse the tomatoes for 30 seconds. Remove and, when cool enough to handle, peel, core, and chop the tomatoes. Combine the tomatoes, onion, mint, vinegar, oil, and salt in a mixing bowl. Taste and adjust seasonings. Serve in small bowls to accompany the chips.

Sopressata Chips

MAKES ONE GOOD-SIZE BOWL CHIPS

1 pound sopressata or other good-quality salami
½ cup finely grated Asiago cheese

Preheat the oven to 325°F.

Purchase pre-cut sopressata or cut into very thin slices using a mandoline. Line a baking sheet with parchment paper, arrange the slices on it, and sprinkle with the cheese. When the sheet is full, cover the slices with another piece of parchment paper, and add another layer of sopressata and cheese. Top with a final layer of parchment. Repeat with another baking sheet, if necessary.

Bake for about 20 minutes or until most of the fat has been rendered from the soppressata. Remove from the oven and transfer the chips to paper towels to drain, blotting any excess oil. Cool completely before serving. These chips can be made the day before the party if stored in an airtight container.

Cheese Straws

MAKES 2 DOZEN STICKS

2 cups all-purpose flour
1 teaspoon salt
2 teaspoons dry mustard
¼ teaspoon cayenne pepper
¾ cup grated cheddar cheese
¾ cup sweet butter, at room temperature
4 tablespoons water
2 egg whites, lightly whisked
1 tablespoon cumin seeds

Preheat the oven to 425°F. Sift the flour, salt, mustard, and cayenne into a medium bowl. In large bowl, combine the cheese and butter with an electric mixer until well blended. Gradually add the flour mixture then the water, and continue to mix for 1 minute. Turn onto a lightly floured surface and knead for 20 seconds. Roll the dough out into a rectangle about 12-by-18 inches. Place on tray or baking sheet and refrigerate for 20 minutes.

When the dough is chilled, cut in half to create two 9-by-12-inch pieces, then cut each half into 24 strips. Twist the strips so they're shaped like licorice sticks, and arrange on a nonstick baking sheet. Brush lightly with egg whites and sprinkle with cumin seeds. Bake for about 15 minutes or until golden brown. Transfer to a rack to cool. Cheese straws can be stored in an airtight container for up to one week; they will improve in flavor if baked 1 or 2 days before serving.

snowshoe PICNIC

Jerry Thomas is the most famous bartender in the world, though many of us don't know it. Called "The Professor" by his disciples, Mr. Thomas started the recognizable portion of his career as a bartender at the El Dorado resort in San Francisco in the early 1850s. Legend has it that a gun-toting gang burst into the bar one night and demanded all the money. Instead of panicking, Thomas coolly asked them if they would like a drink before moving on. Apparently, the bandits were so taken by his concoctions that they stayed for hours, and soon they were happily lying on the floor so that their guns were easily removed from their persons. At the subsequent hanging, the townspeople begged him for the recipe that had vanquished the criminals, but he refused to part with it, saying he would not serve it again until a similar need arose.

After striking gold and starting a successful minstrel band, Thomas disappears from the record books. The legend is that a miner challenged him to make a drink and it was the first one he had never heard of. On finding out that the beverage in question was native to Central America, he headed south to learn its secrets. In any event, a few years later, he was established in quick succession as principal bartender at two of America's swankiest restaurants: the Planter's House in St. Louis and the Metropolitan Hotel in New York. His 1862 book *How to Mix Drinks or The Bon Vivant's Companion* quickly became the bible for bartenders across the country and still sets the standard for cocktail compendiums of flair and polish.

Though hardly a fair tribute to the Professor's Wild West origins, this sporting picnic in Sun Valley, Idaho, does give a sense of how one might adapt his deliciously adventurous spirit to contemporary partying. He, more than anyone we know of, set the standard for a combination of spontaneous living and polished mixology. Why not strap a party on to your back and climb to the top of a nearby mountain, have a few drinks and tasty bites with friends against a backdrop of spectacular views, and then snowboard all the way down. Doesn't sound too bad, does it?

extreme drink

The Professor was also famous for creating countless cocktails. His most dramatic and notorious was called the Blue Blazer. It involved two large pewter beer mugs, and four ounces scotch mixed with four ounces boiling water and two sugar cubes. He would pour the mixture into one of the mugs, dim the lights, light it on fire, and pour the flaming mixture from one mug to the other until the flame went out. An engraving in his *Bon Vivant's Companion* shows him with each arm fully outstretched, a mug in each hand, and a blue lightning bolt shooting between them. He was certainly not one to shy away from the dramatic, and we insist that in his honor you try this at least once. It may well change the way you think to drink.

food to go

When throwing parties on the go, apply the rules of the most traditional cocktail party fare. Make everything finger friendly (not too greasy, not too messy), and don't let it be unwieldly. When packing foods, separate layers with parchment or wax paper, and don't forget the napkins.

paper or plastic?

Never, is the answer. Not only are these materials wasteful, using glass, linen, and silver makes any event hugely better. Plastic cups are the death of any true cocktail. So, even if you are on top of a mountain, take that extra step to serve your guests in nothing but the best.

DRINKS

Steamy Dream, 2000

FOR THE DRINKS:
2 ounces dark rum
½ ounce fresh lemon juice
3 ounces hot water
½ ounce Ginger-Cinnamon Syrup
Cinnamon stick for garnish

FOR THE GINGER-CINNAMON SYRUP:
1 cup sugar
1 cup water
4 inches fresh gingerroot, peeled and chopped
3 cinnamon sticks

To make the flavored syrup, combine the sugar, water, gingerroot, and cinnamon sticks in a saucepan over low heat. Stir until the sugar dissolves, then allow the mixture to come to a low boil for 5 minutes. Remove from heat and cool. Strain, discarding the gingerroot and cinnamon sticks.

Combine the rum, lemon juice, hot water, and flavored syrup in a heat-resistant glass. Serve with a cinnamon swizzle stick.

Hot Dixie Chocolate, 2002

2 ounces bourbon
2 ounces good-quality semisweet chocolate
1 cup whole milk
2 tablespoons heavy cream
½ teaspoon vanilla
1 teaspoon sugar

Finely chop the chocolate and set it aside in a small bowl.

In a small saucepan over low heat, combine the milk, heavy cream, vanilla, and sugar, stirring until the sugar has dissolved and the milk is very hot but not boiling. Remove from heat, pour the milk mixture over the chocolate pieces, and let stand for a minute or two or until the chocolate has melted. Add the bourbon, stirring well to combine. Serve steaming hot in a heat-resistant glass.

NOTE: If you rewarm this drink, do not allow to boil.
(For photo, see page 121.)

Tangerine Margarita

This is yet another marvelous variation on the standard that takes advantage of seasonal citrus.

1½ ounces tequila
½ ounce Cointreau
1½ ounces fresh tangerine juice (see Fresh Fruit Juice, page 33)
¾ ounce fresh orange juice
½ ounce fresh lime juice
Tangerine slices for garnish

Place the tequila, Cointreau, tangerine, orange, and lime juices, and plenty of cracked ice in a shaker, and shake vigorously to combine. Strain into a well-chilled cocktail glass, and serve with the tangerine slices as a garnish.
(For photo, see page 123.)

FOOD

Pear and Chèvre Cheese Puffs

MAKES 8 PIECES

4 ripe pears (about 2 pounds)
3 tablespoons sweet butter
¼ cup chopped hazelnuts
2 tablespoons dark rum
¼ teaspoon cinnamon
1 pinch cardamom
1 pinch salt
6 ounces frozen puff pastry dough, thawed
¼ pound chèvre cheese
1 egg

Peel the pears and cut into small cubes. In a sauté pan, melt the butter over low heat. Add the hazelnuts and toast, about 2 minutes. Add the pear and sauté until soft, about 8 minutes. Add the rum, cinnamon, cardamom, and salt, stirring to combine, and continue to cook until the liquid evaporates. Remove from heat and set aside.

Preheat the oven to 400°F. On a lightly floured surface, roll out the puff pastry dough until ⅛-inch thick. Using a 4-inch cookie cutter, cut out eight circles. Spread a thin layer of chèvre on each circle of dough then add about 1½ tablespoons pear mixture to the center of each. Whisk the egg in a glass, then brush the edges of the puff pastry circles with the egg. Fold the circles in half, pressing the edges to seal in the filling, and place on a lightly greased or nonstick baking sheet. Brush the top of each pastry with egg, and bake for 15 minutes or until puffy and golden brown. Serve at room temperature or warm.

Smoked Turkey and Black Bread Tea Sandwiches

MAKES 16 SANDWICHES

16 thin slices black bread
5 tablespoons sweet butter, at room temperature
1 pound smoked turkey, thinly sliced
1 medium bunch fresh watercress
8 medium radishes, thinly sliced
Salt to taste

Spread one side of each piece of bread with butter. On eight of the slices, place a thin layer of turkey, a few watercress stalks, and a layer of radish slices. Sprinkle each with salt and top with a second piece of buttered bread. Using a sharp knife, cut off the crusts and cut in half, or use cookie cutters to create decorative shapes. Serve within a few hours.

New Potatoes with Rémoulade

Any kind of boiling potatoes can be used in this recipe but new potatoes are the most delicious and, due to their manageable size, will not have to be cut before eating.

MAKES 12 TO 15 POTATOES PLUS SAUCE

12 to 15 new potatoes (about 2 pounds)

FOR THE RÉMOULADE:
1 egg yolk
1 teaspoon Dijon mustard
¾ cup canola oil
1 teaspoon fresh lemon juice
½ teaspoon grated lemon zest
1 teaspoon chopped fresh parsley
1 teaspoon chopped fresh chives
1 teaspoon chopped fresh tarragon
1 tablespoon chopped capers
4 tablespoons finely chopped dill pickles
Salt and pepper to taste

Wash the potatoes thoroughly. Place unpeeled potatoes in a heavy pot, add water to cover, and boil over medium heat for 20 to 30 minutes or until soft when gently pierced with a fork. Remove from heat, drain, and set aside to cool.

To make the rémoulade, whisk together the egg yolk and mustard until thick. Add the oil slowly, whisking constantly, until it all has been incorporated and the mixture resembles mayonnaise. Stir in the lemon juice, add the lemon zest, parsley, chives, and tarragon, then the capers and pickles, and mix well. Add salt and pepper to taste and refrigerate for at least one hour or up to one week if stored in an airtight container. Serve the chilled rémoulade in a small bowl as an accompaniment to the new potatoes.

(For photo, see page 121.)

Asian-Style
Pork Rice Balls

MAKES 8 PIECES

1½ cups short-grain white rice
2 cups water
3 tablespoons rice vinegar
3 tablespoons sugar
1½ teaspoons salt
2 tablespoons sweet butter
2 tablespoons minced shallot
½ pound ground pork
1 teaspoon cider vinegar
2 teaspoons brown sugar
2 tablespoons finely chopped *shiso leaf**
4 sheets *wakame* seaweed*

*Available at Asian grocers or specialty food stores

Wash and thoroughly rinse the rice. Place the water and rice in a heavy pot, and soak for 30 minutes. Cover, bring to a boil over high heat, then quickly reduce the heat to low. Cook for 15 minutes or until the water has completely evaporated. Transfer to a mixing bowl. Combine the rice vinegar, sugar, and 1½ teaspoons salt in a small glass. Pour the vinegar mixture into the rice, stirring constantly, but be careful not to crush the rice grains. Place a damp towel over the rice and set aside to cool.

Melt the butter in a skillet over medium heat, sauté the shallots for 2 minutes, then add the pork. Cook for 10 minutes, using a wooden spoon to break up the meat, or until the pork is completely browned. Stir in the cider vinegar, brown sugar, and 1 teaspoon salt, then remove from heat. Cool to room temperature, then add the *shiso* and mix.

Toast the *wakame* over low heat by holding sheets 6 inches above the flame, gently moving them back and forth to prevent burning. It should take only 3 to 5 seconds to toast each side. Cut the toasted sheets in half, then in half again so you have 16 squares.

To assemble the rice balls, fill a bowl with warm water. Dip your hands in the water and dry lightly on a damp towel. Roll 2-inch ball of rice. Make an indent into the center of the ball and fill with about 2 tablespoons pork mixture. Roll again to cover the pork with the rice. With damp hands, place the rice ball on top of a piece of *wakame*. Place a second piece on top of the rice ball, at an angle to the first. Shape the *wakame* around the rice. If the seaweed starts to crack, dip your hands in water and wet it. Rinse your hands in the water, drying lightly, and repeat until you have 8 large rice balls. Arrange on a platter and serve immediately.

HOLIDAY fête

the details

We don't know about God, but a party is certainly in the details. Here are just a few things people forget:

THE BATHROOM: Give your guests a space to relax and freshen up. Provide lavender or lemon-scented facial spritzer, breath mints, extra toilet paper, tampons, a hand mirror, lipstick, scented candles, and flowers.

COAT-HANGING SPACE: Have plenty of hangers or rent a rack or use a bedroom—just make sure to plan ahead so you can direct people where to put their coats. If it's raining, provide a place for wet umbrellas.

ASHTRAYS: If you allow smoking, place ashtrays on all the side tables unless you like cleaning cigarettes out of glasses at the end of the evening.

COCKTAIL NAPKINS: No one likes a sticky finger.

Alexandra grew up on a small farm in Vermont, about as far from Eliot's Manhattan childhood digs as one can imagine, at least in terms of lifestyle. After fleeing from Boston society in the early sixties, her family raised their own animals and grew their own food on a few hundred acres of rolling hills. Her mother was the "egg lady" for the tiny town. They hung sides of beef from a large hook in the living room before carving them. A goat that had been injured and nursed back to health by one of her sisters lived with them in the house for a number of years.

When not farming, her father helped out on the volunteer fire department and her mother worked at the local food co-op. They knew everyone in town. They became famous (if you can be famous in a Vermont farming village) for their annual holiday party. The whole town would come up the hill each year and let 'er rip. There was moonlight sledding down the long driveway and ice skating on the pond. Cars repeatedly got stuck in the snow and delegations were sent out to free them. The Christmas tree blazed with real candles.

The other houses were too far away to go caroling, and it was always much too cold anyway, so they would just sing to each other. Invariably, toward the end of the night, the furniture was carried outside and the whole party was on the dance floor, if not till dawn then considerably later than they had been up the rest of the year. In memory of this good, old-fashioned holiday fun that wasn't afraid to break a few rules, we created this party.

unhired help:
friends and family

When you give a party, enlist support.
Early guests generally prefer to help than be
served. Though this is something we have
never understood, it seems to set them at
ease. It will also help you get things done in
the crucial minutes when the party is getting
underway. Here are just a few things they
can do:

● **Ask a friend to pass hors d'oeuvres—
this is a great way for them to meet people.**

● **Let a few people know the details of what
you are serving and who is coming; they can
help host if you are otherwise occupied at
the door.**

● **Tell a gregarious friend to help make introductions and keep the conversation flowing.**

DRINKS

Moroccan Knight, 2002

This is a rich variation on a red wine sangria. It is wonderful served in a punch bowl and best if made an hour or so in advance to allow time for the flavors to mingle.

FOR THE SANGRIA:

4 ounces red wine
1 ounce brandy
1 ounce Cardamom-Honey Syrup
1 ounce fresh lemon juice
Lemon peel for garnish

FOR THE CARDAMOM-HONEY SYRUP:

¼ cup honey
½ cup water
4 lemon peel twists
2 tablespoons dried cardamom pods

To make the flavored syrup, place the honey, water, lemon twists, and cardamom pods in a small saucepan. Stir over low heat until the honey dissolves, about 15 minutes. Remove from heat and cool. Strain, reserving the lemon twists for the garnish.

Combine the red wine, brandy, flavored syrup, and fresh lemon juice in a wine glass, and stir well. Garnish with the lemon twist and serve.

Cassis Cocktail

Here's another forgotten mix of yore that guests will enjoy.

2 ounces bourbon
¼ ounce cassis
½ ounce crème de cassis
Lemon peel for garnish

Place the bourbon, cassis, and crème de cassis in a shaker, along with plenty of cracked ice, and shake vigorously to combine. Rub the rim of a cocktail glass with the lemon peel and strain the contents of the shaker into the glass. Garnish with the lemon peel and serve.

Boatswain's Brew, 1999

FOR THE BREW:
1 ounce cognac
3 ounces jasmine tea
½ ounce Vanilla Bean Syrup
½ ounce fresh lemon juice
Fresh ginger and lemon slices

FOR THE VANILLA BEAN SYRUP:
2 vanilla beans
1 cup sugar
1 cup water

To make flavored syrup, combine the vanilla beans, sugar, and water in a saucepan. Stir over low heat, until the sugar has dissolved, about 15 minutes. Remove from heat to cool. Strain, discarding the vanilla beans.

Put the tea, flavored syrup, lemon juice, and fresh ginger and lemon slices in a saucepan, and stir over low heat until hot but not boiling. Pour into a heat-resistant glass, add the cognac, and stir. Garnish with slices of ginger and lemon and serve.

(For photo, see page 132.)

FOOD

Lacy Pancakes with Persimmon Relish

MAKES 16 PIECES

FOR THE RELISH:
2 tablespoons sweet butter
½ cup chopped onion
1 tablespoon Cointreau
1 tablespoon cider vinegar
6 ripe Hachiya (or Japanese) persimmons
 (about 2½ pounds), skinned and chopped
½ teaspoon salt

FOR THE PANCAKES:
8 large eggs

To make the relish, melt the butter in a saucepan over medium heat. Add the onion and cook until soft, about 5 minutes. Turn the heat to high, and stir in the Cointreau and vinegar. Simmer for 30 seconds, then remove from heat. Add the persimmons and salt and toss to combine. Set aside.

To make the pancakes, beat the eggs in a medium bowl. Heat a nonstick skillet over medium heat. In the meantime, transfer the beaten eggs to a turkey baster (keep your finger over the end or the batter will leak out!), and squirt one pancake into the pan in a thin stream, keeping the baster moving to create a lacelike effect. Cook the pancake until it is lightly golden on top, about 1 minute, then flip over and cook briefly, about 10 seconds. Transfer the pancake to a plate, and repeat until all the batter has been used.

On a flat surface, cut the pancakes in half. Place 2 to 3 tablespoons persimmon relish in the middle of each half, wrap the pancake around the relish, and turn over to keep the contents from spilling out. Serve just slightly warm.

(For photo, see page 131.)

Pork-and-Veal Pâté on Apple Slices

MAKES 16 PIECES OR ABOUT 1½ CUPS PÂTÉ PLUS APPLE SLICES FOR DIPPING

1 pound ground pork shoulder
½ pound ground veal shoulder
1 small onion, finely chopped
¼ cup black Mission figs, pitted and chopped
1 cup water
¼ cup cognac
½ pound salt pork, finely chopped
1 tablespoon maple syrup
¼ teaspoon ground cloves
¼ teaspoon cinnamon
Freshly ground black pepper to taste
2 medium apples (we like Fuji)
3 teaspoons fresh lemon juice

Place the ground pork, ground veal, onion, figs, and water in a large nonstick pot over medium heat. Cook, breaking up the meat with a wooden spoon, until the water evaporates and the meat begins to fry, about 25 minutes. Adjust the heat to high, add the cognac, and cook until it evaporates, about 5 minutes.

In the meantime, cook the salt pork in a medium saucepan over medium heat, stirring occasionally, until fat is rendered and the pork is golden brown, about 30 minutes.

Add the salt pork and rendered fat to the meat mixture in the large pot and combine over medium heat. Add the maple syrup, cloves, cinnamon, and pepper to taste, and mix well.

Transfer the pâté to a bowl, cover, and set aside to cool. Refrigerate for at least 2 hours before serving. When ready to serve, cut the apples into 16 slices and sprinkle with the lemon juice. Serve the pâté spread on the apple slices or allow your guests to serve themselves.

Chestnuts with Toasted Pecans

MAKES ABOUT 24 PIECES

1 pound fresh chestnuts
2 cups milk
2 cups water
2 tablespoons sweet butter
½ cup finely ground pecans
½ teaspoon salt

Preheat the oven to 425°F. With a sharp knife, cut an X on the flat side of each chestnut. Place the chestnuts on a baking sheet and roast for 15 to 20 minutes. Cool thoroughly, then remove the dark brown outer shells and the bitter inner skins. Set aside.

In a saucepan over medium heat, combine the milk and water and bring to a low boil. Add the peeled chestnuts and cook until tender, about 20 minutes. Strain, discarding the cooking liquid, and set aside. Preheat the broiler.

Melt the butter in a saucepan over low heat, then add the pecans and salt and sauté until lightly browned, about 5 minutes. Transfer to a flat surface and roll the peeled chestnuts in the toasted pecans to coat thoroughly. Place the coated chestnuts on a lightly oiled baking sheet and broil until toasty brown, 1 to 2 minutes. Skewer with toothpicks and serve warm.

Cranberry–Almond Biscotti

MAKES 20–25 COOKIES

1 cup sweetened dried cranberries
1 cup whole almonds
2 cups flour
1½ cups sugar
½ teaspoon baking powder
½ teaspoon baking soda
½ teaspoon salt
3 large eggs plus 1 egg white
1 teaspoon vanilla extract
½ teaspoon cinnamon
1 tablespoon sweet butter

Preheat the oven to 325°F. Soak the cranberries in hot water until soft, about 30 minutes. Drain and set aside. In the meantime, spread the almonds on a nonstick baking sheet and toast until deep brown, about 10 minutes. Cool thoroughly, roughly chop, and set aside. Do not turn off the oven.

Combine the flour, sugar, baking powder, baking soda, and salt in a mixing bowl. In a small bowl, whisk the three eggs with the vanilla and cinnamon. Pour the egg mixture into the flour mixture, and mix thoroughly using a wooden spoon until a dough forms. Add the cranberries and almonds to the dough and mix well.

Turn the dough out onto a floured counter or board and divide into flattened loaves, about 3 by 12 inches each. Butter and flour a baking sheet, transfer the loaves to the sheet, and brush lightly with the egg white. Bake for 25 to 30 minutes or until the loaves are golden brown and fragrant. Remove from the oven to cool, but do not turn off the oven.

To shape the biscotti, cut the cooled loaves on a diagonal into ¾-inch-thick slices. Lay the slices on the baking sheet and bake for another 20 minutes or until toasted and crisp. Cool thoroughly before serving or transfer to an airtight container for up to 2 weeks.

all-night BLOW OUT

The society balls of the past few centuries are hard for us to imagine. "A ball is the only social function in America to which such qualifying words as splendor and magnificence can with proper modesty of expression be applied," wrote Emily Post, in her 1922 first edition of *Etiquette*. Though "modesty of expression" may not exactly apply to Post herself, she is right on the money about the supreme importance of the ball in the history of American partying. The attention we give now to what people are wearing at major events and who flirts with who pales in comparison.

These were events for which all the social families in the major cities up and down the East coast would prepare for months. They were the absolute height of elegance. When the big night arrived, the entire estate was filled with enormously palpable excitement. Several generations, old and young alike, would dance and mingle almost the whole of the night, have a light breakfast at four, and then be whisked away in carriages as the sun was rising.

What happened to us? It used to be a matter of course that for a special event we would be up almost all night. Not merely the virile nymphs of nineteen but people of all ages were simply transfixed by the fun and splendor of the festivities. The only comparable contemporary event is the gala, but these affairs tend to end rather early. So where do you go after it ends on one of those rare nights when everything seems possible? Everyone is dressed up and in terrific spirits, and the benefit or opening invariably ends earlier than your group is ready for. Why not invite them over for a drink? It will make everyone's night and takes much less preparation than you would think. In fact, we keep a regular arsenal of entertaining staples on hand for just this type of occasion. So, next time, whoop it up and make a night of it that would do your forebears proud.

being a good host

It's very simple: comfortable guests make happy guests. Guests will not be comfortable unless the host is. So:

● Relax and smile—enjoy yourself or no one else will.

● Greet people at the door—this is the chief duty of any host.

● Offer them a drink right away (or walk them to the bar if it is self-service), and immediately introduce them to someone.

● Don't spend all your time in the kitchen or behind the bar—even if your guests didn't come to see you, they need you around to feel comfortable.

getting people to **leave**

In Hitchcock's *Notorious*, Ingrid Bergman has the best party-closing line in history. The hostess of a small gathering, she decides she wants to spend the rest of the evening with a particularly dashing Cary Grant (a choice most of us might make in her place). She scratches the record to a halt, glares at her guests, and belts, "This has been a perfectly hideous party. You all must go."

Unfortunately everyone can't be Ingrid Bergman. Here are some slightly more subtle ways of getting them out when it's time:

- **Close the bar down.**
- **Turn off the music.**
- **Stop being so damn exciting— let the conversation lull.**
- **Drop hints: tell your guests how much you enjoyed having them over.**
- **Say you are tired and put your pajamas on.**
- **Turn off the lights and go to bed.**

drunk drivers
call 911

Everything is going swimmingly, and everyone appears to be having a fantastic time. You are in no way ready to stop. But unless you live in one of a few, taxi-rich cities, your guests have a problem: they have to drive home. As host, you should do your best never to let your guests drive drunk. Instead be prepared to gracefully deflect copious, well-lubricated objections to staying the night. And, remember, a great thing about having friends stay the night is you will have some help cleaning up the next day.

Here are a few things to try:

If you think it may be that kind of evening, let your guests in on your premonition and suggest they take a taxi to the party. Make sure they know who's coming from their area as they may want to ride together.

PROVIDE DETERRENTS. Set out copious amounts of water in places where it is easy for everyone to reach. Small, individual bottles are best as no one has to go routing around for a glass when they need a sip. And provide food—bread and crackers if that is all you have. As we all know, the fastest way to get absolutely silly and inebriated is to drink on an empty stomach.

APPOINT A DESIGNATED DRIVER. Get friends to carpool and have them choose the one amongst themselves who won't imbibe that evening.

HAVE A KEY PARTY. Invite anyone and everyone who wants to let loose to spend the night or ride home in a taxi. As guests arrive, take their keys. Post a list of taxi services by the phone for all to see, then pile all the blankets, sheets, and pillows you own in one room and invite everyone to make themselves at home for the night. Make a bed on the floor to show them how it's done. After all, slumber parties never go out of fashion.

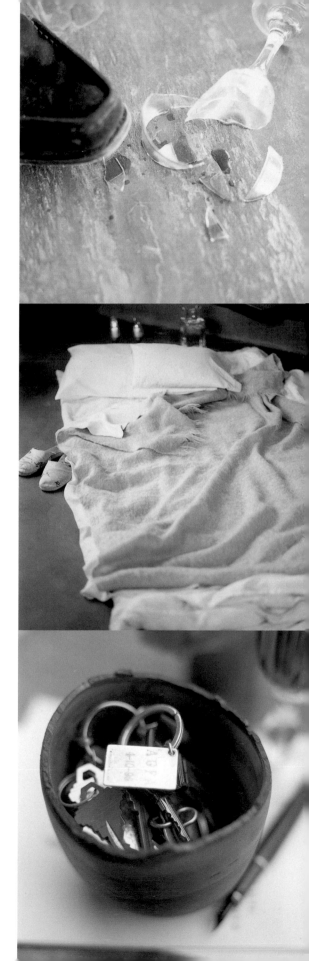

DRINKS

Praying Dame, 2001

1½ ounces light rum
½ ounce maraschino liqueur
1 ounce fresh blood orange juice (see Fresh Fruit Juice, page 33)
½ ounce fresh lemon juice
Blood orange wheel for garnish

Place the rum, maraschino liqueur, blood orange juice, and lemon juice in a shaker, along with plenty of cracked ice, and shake vigorously to combine. Strain thoroughly into a well-chilled cocktail glass. Garnish with the blood orange wheel and serve.
(For photo, see pages 139 and 143.)

Maiden's Blush, 2000

1 ounce vodka
½ ounce Limoncello
1 ounce fresh tangerine juice (see Fresh Fruit Juice, page 33)
½ ounce pomegranate juice

Combine all the ingredients in a shaker, along with plenty of cracked ice, and shake vigorously to combine. Strain thoroughly into a well-chilled cocktail glass and serve.
(For photo, see page 139.)

Zoot Suit, 2001

1 ounce tequila
1 ounce Alizé
1½ ounces fresh passion fruit juice (see Fresh Fruit Juice, page 33)
1 teaspoon fresh lime juice
Superfine sugar to taste (optional)
Passion fruit seeds for garnish

Place the tequila, Alizé, passion fruit juice and lime juice, and plenty of cracked ice in a shaker, and shake vigorously to combine. For sweet tooths, you may want to add a teaspoon or more of superfine sugar to the shaker, then shake again. Strain thoroughly into a well-chilled cocktail glass, and garnish with a few passion fruit seeds.

Negroni

This may have been named for a Count Negroni of Florence who, supposedly, was so well known in local taverns that devotees christened his drink of choice after him. Regardless, it is a great old Italian cocktail.

1 ounce gin
1 ounce Campari
1 ounce vermouth
Lemon peel for garnish
Soda water (optional)

Place the gin, Campari, and vermouth in a shaker, along with plenty of cracked ice, and shake vigorously to combine. Strain into a well-chilled cocktail glass, and garnish with the lemon twist. For those who prefer this drink a bit lighter, top it with a splash of soda water.

FOOD

Pigs in a Blanket

Use high-quality hot dogs and Dijon mustard for a more adult version of this childhood favorite. We like Niman Ranch's Hot Dogs, available at specialty food stores or nimanranch.com.

MAKES 24 PIECES

16 ounces frozen pastry dough, thawed
6 good-quality hot dogs
6 thin slices Havarti cheese
Dijon mustard for dipping

Preheat the oven to 425°F. Roll the pastry dough out until ⅛-inch thick, then slice into 6 equal pieces. Slit the hot dogs in half, lengthwise. Place a slice of cheese in between each pair, then put the halves back together. Roll each cheese-dog in pastry dough, covering both ends and pressing them together so the "blanket" is sealed. Transfer to a lightly oiled baking sheet and bake for 15 minutes, or until browned. Slice each pig in a blanket into four pieces, and serve on a platter with mustard for dipping.

Offer guests toothpicks or present as finger food.

Trio of Breadsticks

When planning a long night, be sure to offer foods that are a bit heavy and oily, like these breadsticks and tapenade. By coating the stomach, these hors d'oeuvres will help slow down inebriation and counteract the alcohol's acidity. If you don't have time to make the recipes below, offer some good, store-bought bread served with a variety of flavored butters and oils for dipping, such as olive butter and basil-garlic olive oil.

MAKES 3 DOZEN

FOR THE BREADSTICKS:
1 teaspoon active dry yeast
1 cup warm water
1 tablespoon honey
6 tablespoons extra-virgin olive oil
3 cups all-purpose flour
Sea salt for seasoning

FOR THE FLAVORING AGENTS:
1 tablespoon grated orange zest
2 tablespoons finely chopped toasted pine nuts
2 tablespoons toasted fennel seeds

Combine the yeast with ¼ cup warm water and set aside to proof. In a separate bowl, combine the honey and remaining water, stirring until the honey is dissolved. Add 3 tablespoons olive oil to the mixture, then stir the honey-oil mixture into the yeast and set aside.

Brush three medium bowls with olive oil and set aside. In a mixing bowl, combine the flour and salt.

Add the honey-oil mixture and combine with your hands until a dough forms. Transfer the dough to a floured surface and pull off one third. Return the remaining two thirds to the large bowl. Add the orange zest to the first third of the dough, knead for 5 to 8 minutes, then form a ball. Transfer to one of the oiled bowls and cover with a towel. Split the remaining dough in half, add the pine nuts to one piece and the fennel seeds to the other, and repeat the process so that you have three kinds of dough. Set the covered bowls in a warm place for an hour to an hour and a half, until the dough has doubled in size.

When the first batch of dough is ready, transfer to a lightly floured surface, knead it a few times, then cut into twelve equal pieces. Roll each of the pieces into 12-inch-long sticks. Place the sticks on a lightly oiled baking sheet with about one inch between them. Cover with a light towel and return to a warm place to rise for 20 to 30 more minutes. Preheat the oven to 425°F, then repeat the process with the remaining two batches of dough.

When ready to bake, lightly brush each batch of breadsticks with the remaining 3 tablespoons olive oil and sprinkle very lightly with the sea salt. Bake until the breadsticks just begin to brown, about 12 minutes. Cool on wire racks and serve immediately, or store in airtight containers for up to 3 days before serving.

Tapenade

MAKES 1½ CUPS

2 egg yolks
1 tablespoon spicy brown mustard
2 tablespoons fresh lemon juice
1 tablespoon vinegar
1 teaspoon salt
1 teaspoon sugar
¾ cup good-quality olive oil
8 ounces oil-cured black olives, pitted and minced
    (about 8 tablespoons)
2 tablespoons minced capers
1 tablespoon chopped chives
1 tablespoon fresh chopped parsley
½ teaspoon grated lemon zest

Rinse the container of a blender with hot water to warm it. Add the egg yolks, mustard, lemon juice, vinegar, salt, and sugar, and blend for 5 to 10 seconds until well combined. With the motor still running, slowly add the oil in a steady stream. Transfer to a bowl, then stir in the olives, capers, chives, parsley, and lemon zest until thoroughly combined. Taste and adjust seasonings. Serve immediately or refrigerate for several hours before the party.

Seasoned Edamame

Fresh soybeans, or edamame, sprinkled with salt are a frequent accompaniment to cocktails in Japan—just peel and eat! Edamame are available frozen at most good grocery stores.

MAKES ONE GOOD-SIZE BOWL

1 tablespoon plus 2 teaspoons kosher salt
One 16-ounce package frozen edamame
1 teaspoon crushed pink peppercorns

Boil water in a pot, add 1 tablespoon salt and the edamame, and cook for 4 to 5 minutes, or until the beans are tender. Drain the beans, then immediately immerse in a bowl of ice water. Cool for 3 minutes, then thoroughly drain again. Transfer to a serving bowl and toss with the remaining salt and the pepper. Remember to provide guests with an extra bowl where they can discard the soybean shells.

the **DAY**
after

Simple pleasures. A fresh cup of coffee.

A massage. The Sunday *New York Times*. A good book that you've been neglecting. Breakfast with an old friend. A walk in the park where you actually look at the trees. Lying in bed with your dog. Or your lover. Or both. There are countless things we love to do yet take for granted, and consequently do not do frequently, or fully, enough.

So take your time. Enjoy your morning. Enjoy yourself. Think of all the fun you had. If friends stayed over, all the better. Turn the morning cleanup into a little bit of a celebration. Take some extra time to review the night before with them. Who did something crazy? Who looked fantastic? What was beautiful? But take care to remember that parties are about simple pleasures, just as beautiful mornings are.

"I can think of nothing less pleasurable than a life devoted to pleasure," said that captain of hedonism John D. Rockefeller. Though we hardly agree with Mr. Rockefeller—and can think of a few things worse than a life devoted to pleasure—there is something to the fact that the occasional pleasure, the unexpected pleasure, the spontaneous pleasure can be more affecting and beautiful than something that we do everyday. This is what parties represent to both of us. The best of pleasures. We hope this book in some way helps you feel the same.

disco kitchen

Inspired by a friend of Alexandra's parents during that fleeting, golden era when Michael Jackson's *Thriller* was topping the charts, this is a surefire way to get all the morning-after cleaning done and leave everyone in a good mood. Put on some fine dancing music, blast the stereo, and get everyone scrubbing.

cleaning up

RED WINE STAINS: Blot up excess wine quickly. Wet thoroughly with soda water and cover with salt. Allow to sit for 10 minutes. Dabbing with hydrogen peroxide may help, as will putting the stained item in a sink or bowl then pouring boiling water over it from a height of two to three feet.

AIRING OUT: Empty all the ashtrays and clean up dirty glasses before going to bed. Open all the windows. The place will smell better and the fresh air will help you wake up feeling somewhat better. Also try incense, scented candles, and room spray.

FRUIT JUICE STAINS: Use cold water to rinse first. Blot with a sponge (do not rub). Do not use soap except as a last resort because it will often cause the stain to set. If possible, put the stained item in a bowl, then pour boiling water over the stain from a height of two to three feet.

ALCOHOL STAINS ON WOODEN FURNITURE: These can be very tricky to treat since alcohol dissolves many finishes. First, when possible, clean up immediately and rub with an oiled cloth. If found the next day or the next week, use one of the few good products available to help you with the task.

WATER STAINS ON WOOD: Prevent this from happening by keeping furniture well polished. Otherwise, if it does, rub wood with a dampened cloth sprinkled with a few drops of peppermint oil.

LIGHT SCRATCHES ON WOOD: Polish the area and if that doesn't work, rub carefully inside the scratch with a piece of walnut meat, which colors the wood brown.

VOTIVE WAX: Clean out votives of leftover wax by putting them in a freezer overnight. Once frozen, the wax will easily crack out and the votives can be washed with hot water to remove any excess.

WAX DRIPPINGS: Scrape up with a credit card. Remove from a carpet by covering the area with a brown paper bag and ironing until the wax separates.

SMOKE SMELL: Immerse a bath towel in cold water, wring it out, and then slop and swish it around the room.

hangovers

The best way to avoid a terrible hangover is to
stop tippling as long as possible before bed
(though for some of us, these two events are
simultaneous) and drink lots and lots of water.
Take an aspirin or two to avoid the evil
headache and shakes.

Salty french fries, a cheeseburger, and a Coke
the next morning is our preferred hangover
treatment, although the hair of the dog, a nice
restorative drink like a spicy Bloody Mary, does
wonders and wonders and wonders. But the
fact is you are dehydrated, alcohol is a toxin,
and what you need is lots of water and rest.

DRINKS

Fresh Water

You will want lots of this refreshing drink both before and after the party. Drink it chilled, without ice.

½ cucumber, peeled and sliced
8 fresh thyme sprigs
1 large lemon, cut into wheels

Combine all the ingredients in a large pitcher and fill with water. Cover and refrigerate for a few hours before serving.

(For photo, see page 151.)

Best Bloody Mary with Cherry-Tomato Ice

FOR THE ICE CUBES:
6 small cherry tomatoes

FOR THE DRINKS:
2 ounces vodka
4 ounces Clamato (tomato-clam juice)
½ ounce fresh lemon juice
2–3 dashes Worcestershire sauce
2–3 drops Tabasco Sauce
2 teaspoons prepared horseradish
¼ teaspoon celery seeds
Salt and pepper to taste
Celery sticks for garnish

To make the cherry-tomato ice cubes, place one tomato in each compartment of an ice tray. Fill with water and freeze.

Combine the vodka, Clamato, lemon juice, Worcestershire, Tabasco, horseradish, celery seeds, and salt and pepper in a shaker, along with plenty of cracked ice, and shake vigorously to combine.

Fill a water goblet or highball glass with the cherry-tomato ice cubes, then strain the Bloody Mary mix over the glass to fill. Garnish with a celery stick and serve.

Champagne-and-Mint Granita

Make this granita the night of the party using all the uncorked champagne. It is sure to get you on the right track the next day.

SERVES 8

2 cups champagne
2 ounces vodka
1¾ cups water
¾ cup sugar
2 ounces fresh orange juice
2 ounces fresh lemon juice
Peel of one lemon
Peel of one orange
20 fresh mint sprigs plus more for garnish

In a medium saucepan, combine the water, sugar, orange juice, lemon juice, lemon and orange rinds, and half the mint. Boil softly over low heat for about 8 minutes, stirring to dissolve the sugar, then remove from heat. Add the remaining mint to the saucepan, stirring to combine, and set aside to cool.

When the syrup is cool, strain into a large bowl, discarding the mint. Add the champagne and vodka and stir to combine. Pour the mixture into a plastic container large enough so that the liquid is no deeper than an inch. Freeze until slushy—anywhere from 30 minutes to 2 hours.

When the mixture is slushy, remove from the freezer and whisk to well-combine, then return to freezer to freeze thoroughly. When it's almost time to serve, transfer the granita to the refrigerator for about 10 minutes to soften slightly. Serve in champagne glasses or small bowls, and garnish with sprigs of mint.

(For photo, see page 151.)

Frenet Branca Cocktail

This drink may be a bit strong for the weary, but *The Savoy Cocktail Book*, first published in 1930, claims that Frenet Branca is a sure-fire headache cure, and, "one of the best morning-after cocktails ever invented."

2 ounces gin
1 ounce vermouth
1 ounce Frenet Branca

Combine all the ingredients in a shaker, with plenty of cracked ice, and shake vigorously to mix. Strain into a well-chilled cocktail glass and . . . bottoms up.

Pineapple-and-Green-Tea Protein Shake

For those times when you need a real pick-me-up but cannot manage more than a liquid breakfast.

SERVES 1 TO 2

1 cup strong green tea (preferably Macha or other
**   high-quality powdered tea), cooled**
1 cup fresh pineapple juice
½ cup fresh pineapple chunks
1 large ripe banana
2 tablespoons soy powder
6 ice cubes

Combine all the ingredients in a blender and puree. Pour into large glasses and drink up.

FOOD

Bacon–and–Cheddar Strata

Strata is a perfect "day-after" meal because it can be assembled the day before, put in the refrigerator, then popped in the oven when you (finally) roll out of bed. If you don't have time to prepare it the night before, do let it sit out for an hour or so before baking to let the flavors meld.

We developed this *strata* recipe to include plenty of bacon because we often crave this hearty, salty meat after a hard night. Feel free to vary the filling ingredients to fit your preferences.

SERVES 6

8 slices crusty white bread
1 cup boiled spinach
½ pound bacon
2 tablespoons sweet butter
½ cup minced onion
½ cup white wine
1 cup grated cheddar cheese
6 large eggs
¾ cup heavy cream
¾ cup milk
1 teaspoon salt
½ teaspoon black pepper

If the bread is not stale, toast the slices in a 300°F oven until quite crisp, then set aside. Squeeze out any excess water from the spinach, roughly chop, then set aside.

In a skillet over medium heat, fry the bacon until just cooked, then transfer to a paper towel–lined plate and crumble into small pieces. Drain the skillet of almost all the bacon grease, then return it to medium heat. Add 1 tablespoon butter to the skillet, and when it's melted, add the onions and the crumbled bacon, cooking until the onions are translucent, about 2 minutes. Transfer the bacon-onion mixture to a bowl, and set aside. Return the skillet to the stovetop, add the white wine, and over high heat, simmer until reduced by half. Remove from heat and set aside.

Butter an 8-inch-square baking dish and arrange about half the bread to cover the bottom of the dish. Top with half the bacon-onion mixture, then half the spinach, and a third of the cheese. Add the rest of the bread, bacon-onion mixture, and spinach in layers, then another third of the cheese, reserving the last third for later.

In a mixing bowl, whisk the eggs, then whisk in the reduced wine, cream, milk, salt, and pepper. Pour the egg mixture evenly over the layers in the baking dish. Cover the dish tightly with plastic wrap, and refrigerate for at least 1 hour and or overnight.

About 15 minutes before cooking time, remove the baking dish from the refrigerator and preheat the oven to 325°F. Remove the plastic wrap, and sprinkle the remaining ⅓ cup cheese over the top of the *strata*. Bake for about 50 minutes, or until the *strata* is puffy and the cheese has melted. Serve warm.

Blackberry–Orange Muffins

MAKES 12 MUFFINS

4 tablespoons sweet butter
2 cups all-purpose flour
1 tablespoon baking powder
½ teaspoon salt
1 large egg
¾ cup sugar
½ cup milk
¾ cup sour cream
1½ cups frozen blackberries
1 tablespoon grated orange zest

Preheat the oven to 350°F. Lightly grease a 12-cup muffin tin. Melt the butter in a saucepan over low heat, and set aside.

Mix the flour, baking powder, and salt in a medium bowl. In another bowl, whisk the egg, then add the sugar and whisk until thick and thoroughly combined. Continue to whisk, adding the milk and melted butter. Add the sour cream and stir to combine. Fold the egg mixture into the flour mixture until well combined. Add the blackberries and orange zest and stir until just combined.

Drop tablespoons of the batter into the muffin tins until half full, then bake for 35 minutes or until a toothpick inserted into the muffins comes out clean. Cool the muffins in the tins for 10 minutes, then turn out onto a wire rack to finish cooling. Serve immediately or store in an airtight container for up to 2 days.

index

(page numbers in *italic* refer to illustrations.)

credits

Cover: Maple tray available at Crate & Barrel,
 www.crateandbarrel.com

Page 3: Barbara Barry decanters and martini glass available
 through Baccarat, (800) 777-0100, www.baccarat.fr.com

Page 8: Decanter and martini glasses available through
 Takashimaya, (212) 350-0100

Page 14: Martini glasses, tumblers, and Collins glasses
 available at Takashimaya, (212) 350-0100

Page 16: Simon Pearce martini glass available through
 G. F. MacGregor, (207) 596-6300

Page 21: Barbara Barry martini glass and champagne flutes
 available through Baccarat, (800) 777-0100,
 www.baccarat.fr.com

Page 53: Tempo tumblers available at Crate and Barrel,
 www.crateandbarrel.com

Page 57: Martini glass available at Pottery Barn,
 www.potterybarn.com

Page 61: Tempo highball glasses available at Crate and
 Barrel, www.crateandbarrel.com

Page 67: Flowers by Floral Art, (310) 392-1633

Page 73: Punch bowl available at G. F. MacGregor,
 (207) 596-6300

Page 81: Glasses available at Restoration Hardware,
 (800) 762-1005

Page 82: Decanter available at Takashimaya, (212) 350-0100

Pages 87–90: Martini glasses, decanter, and ice bucket
 available at Takashimaya, (212) 350-0100

Pages 98–102: Hula juice glasses available at Crate and
 Barrel, www.crateandbarrel.com

Pages 107–113: Location–The Echo, 1822 Sunset Blvd.,
 Los Angeles, (213) 413-8200

Page 111: Flowers and container by Floral Art,
 (310) 392-1633

Pages 120–123: Simon Pearce tumblers, mugs, and bowls
 available through G. F. MacGregor, (207) 596-6300

Page 128: Simon Pearce martini and wine glasses available
 through G. F. MacGregor, (207) 596-6300

Text copyright © 2002 Alexandra and Eliot Angle
Photography copyright © 2002 Ericka McConnell

Project editor: Sandra Gilbert
Production manager: Kim Tyner
Wardrobe stylist: Andrea Portes
Flowers: Jennifer McGarigle, Floral Art

Published by
Stewart, Tabori & Chang
A Company of La Martinière Groupe
115 West 18th Street
New York, NY 10011

Export Sales to all countries except Canada, France,
and French-speaking Switzerland:
Thames and Hudson Ltd.
181A High Holborn
London WC1V 7QX
England

Canadian Distribution:
Canadian Manda Group
One Atlantic Avenue, Suite 105
Toronto, Ontario M6K 3E7
Canada

Library of Congress Cataloging-in-Publication Data

Angle, Alexandra.
  Cocktail parties with a twist : drink+food+style / Alexandra
  and Eliot Angle ; photography by Ericka McConnell.
    p. cm.
  ISBN 1-58479-210-8 (alk. paper)
  1. Cocktails. 2. Appetizers. 3. Cocktail parties. I. Angle,
Eliot. II. Title.
  TX951 .A48 2002
  641.8'74—dc21
                                        2002070689

DESIGN BY NINA BARNETT

The text of this book was composed in Univers.
Printed in Singapore

1 3 5 7 9 10 8 6 4 2
First Printing